GAME
QUERY

GAME
QUERY

Nontrivial Trivia from
the Minds at *The Economist*

Philip Coggan, Josie Delap, Geoffrey Carr,
John Prideaux and Simon Wright

PUBLICAFFAIRS
New York

PublicAffairs
Hachette Book Group
1290 Avenue of the Americas, New York, NY 10104
www.publicaffairsbooks.com
@Public_Affairs

The Economist in Association with Profile Books Ltd. and PublicAffairs

Printed in the United States of America

Originally published in 2017 by Profile Books Ltd. in Great Britain.

First US Edition: July 2018

Published by PublicAffairs, an imprint of Perseus Books, LLC, a subsidiary of Hachette Book Group, Inc. The PublicAffairs name and logo is a trademark of the Hachette Book Group.

Library of Congress Control Number: 2018946409

ISBNs: 978-1-61039-990-6 (paperback original); 978-1-61039-991-3 (ebook)

LSC-C

10 9 8 7 6 5 4 3 2 1

CONTENTS

CONTENTS

THE **ANSWERS**   93

A SEVERE CONTEST

To answer all the questions in this book, you will need to be a polymath. The volume is divided into 12 parts, representing the 12 themed sections of *The Economist*. Each section has 50 questions, making 600 in all. Many people think *The Economist* only covers economics or politics. This is far from the case. As this foreword was being written in June 2017, the latest issue had articles on elephants, Goethe, global football, opioid abuse in Montana, Chinese civil rights lawyers and an obituary for Roxcy O'Neal Bolton, a feminist who campaigned to have storms named after men as well as women.

The questions in the quiz that awaits you are similarly wide-ranging. In fact, they were beyond the wit of any one individual to devise. Several of the authors are members of *The Economist* quiz team, which regularly does battle with other publications under the name "Marginal Futility", an economics joke that our publishers cruelly rejected as a title for the present volume. (At least we fought off their suggestion of "Megabrains".)

Mega or not, the brain of one individual usually contains unexpected treasures, and it is the joy of a quiz to bring them to light. Our business affairs editor once amazed us by knowing the star sign of Justin Bieber. Unexpected lacunae, on the other hand, are galling. The author will never recover from the shame of being defeated in a tiebreak question over the date of the Alamo siege. It was 1836, if you must know, not that it's in the book.

And neither is Mr Bieber. The matter of general knowledge quizzes is often disparaged as "trivia". But in this era of "post-truth" politics, facts are important. Being stumped by the questions is not a failure; it is an opportunity to be better informed. Many of the answers in the back of the book are discursive, explaining the background to the question and some common misconceptions. Polls show that people regularly overestimate figures such as the proportion of immigrants in the population and the amount of money spent on foreign aid; they are also poor at differentiating between risks. Americans are 13.43 times more likely to die from choking on a piece of food than from terrorism, for example.

As a weekly newspaper, we interpret and select the news. Inevitably and openly, that means many of our articles are opinionated. But we aim to back up our opinions with facts; every piece has to survive the rigorous attention of the research department.

The whole process is a collective effort. That's why, ever since The Economist was founded in 1843, it has not featured individual bylines. (An exception is made for our special reports.) Michael Lewis, the author of The Big Short, once said the anonymity of our authors was designed to hide our callow youth; alas, a look at the greying heads in our newsroom proves him wrong.

Just like the paper, this book is a collective effort. A team of five from various editorial departments devised the questions. The rounds don't carry individual bylines but our identities are no secret. The authors are Geoffrey Carr, Philip Coggan, Josie Delap, John Prideaux and Simon Wright. And, just as with each week's issue, everything had to be fact-checked; Lisa Davies of our research team did the honours.

The one thing more enjoyable than getting a tricky question right is knowing that a friend or family member would get it wrong, a fact we had ample opportunity to learn during the composition of this book. Rest assured, none of us could have answered all the questions in the sections we didn't write. That being so, it may seem unnecessary to single out particular questions as difficult—but for those who like an extra challenge, that's what we've done. These "super-hard" questions (and their answers) are clearly marked with a ⚠.

Perhaps it was inevitable that *The Economist* would produce a quiz. Every week its contents page proclaims our desire to take part in "a severe contest between intelligence, which presses forward, and an unworthy, timid ignorance obstructing our progress." These are words to live by. Time to press forward.

Philip Coggan

Q THE QUESTIONS

MENTAL STATES
US

1. How many people signed the **Declaration of Independence**?

2. The original **star-spangled banner**, about which Francis Scott Key wrote his ditty, got a bit battered in the war of 1812. How many of its white stars are still visible?

3. The first notable **uprising in America** by white settlers against the king took place in 1676. What was it called?

4. How many elected presidents failed to win a plurality of the **popular vote**?

 5. Under the Senate's **filibuster rule**, 41 senators can band together and block legislation. Each state has two senators, so the senators representing the 21 least populous states can in theory exercise a veto on legislation. The 21 least populous states combined are home to what percentage of America's population?

6. Who was the **first American president not to own slaves**?

7. *Democracy in America*, published in 1835, is probably the best book written about American politics. Who was the author?

8. The site of the **Battle of Little Big Horn** is in which state?

9. The **gunfight at the OK Corral** took place between the Clanton and McLaury gangs and the Earps and Doc Holliday. What were the names of Wyatt's two brothers who took part in the shootout?

10. The **People's Party** was founded in 1891 and merged with the Democratic Party five years later. How many states did its candidate win in the presidential election of 1892?

11. Who was the **only man** to serve as both president of the United States and chief justice of the Supreme Court?

12. Barack Obama was the last president to win the **Nobel peace prize.** How many other presidents have won the prize?

13. In 1922, **Rebecca Latimer Felton** became the first woman to serve in the Senate. How long was she there?

 14. Barry Goldwater's book, *The Conscience of a Conservative*, which was published in 1960, inspired a failed presidential campaign and became essential reading for a generation of Republicans. But who actually wrote it?

15. In 1967 the *Loving v Virginia* case reached the Supreme Court. What momentous decision came out of it?

16. Which is the **longest river** in the United States?

17. Which state gets the **most annual rainfall**? And which gets the least?

18. Which state produces the **most coal**?

19. Around 28% of **land in America** is owned by the federal government and most of it is administered by four agencies? Can you name them?

20. There is no escape from **federal income tax** but seven states levy no additional income tax. How many can you name?

21. The American National Election Studies asks those who voted in presidential elections to **place the parties on a left–right scale**, with government should provide "many more services" on the left, and government should "reduce spending a lot" on the right. What percentage of voters in 2016 could not place the Democratic and Republican parties correctly on a left–right scale?

22. US spending on **health care per person** is the highest in the OECD. But where does the US rank in the OECD for life expectancy?

23. A long-standing plan for a statue in the town of Dixon, Illinois, where **Ronald Reagan** spent his early years, would have the president dressed in what to commemorate the job he did in the summer?

24. During the first world war what foodstuff was renamed liberty cabbage to avoid it falling afoul of **anti-German feeling**?

25. Which **city was the birthplace** of T. S. Eliot, Chuck Berry and Yogi Berra?

26. Lauren Bacall, Judy Garland, John Lennon and Rudolph Nureyev all lived at one time in the **same apartment complex**. Which one?

27. How many elected **mosquito-control boards** are there in Florida?

28. In how many states does the state still have a **monopoly on sales of liquor**?

29. Link the state to its **licence plate slogan**: a) First in Flight b) Live Free or Die c) America's Dairyland

30. Which is the only state with a **unicameral legislature**, rather than a separate House and Senate?

31. Which is the **longest bridge** in the United States?

32. Boston named what **engineering feat** after Ted Williams, a former left-fielder with the Red Sox?

 33. What were the original names of these **airports**, now named after former presidents? a) Kennedy b) Reagan c) George Bush Intercontinental

34. The Salk Institute in La Jolla, California, is considered the masterpiece of which great **American architect**?

35. Neil Armstrong was the first American to **walk on the moon**. Who was the last?

36. Which state has the **highest life expectancy**?

37. When, according to Gallup, did the majority of Americans first agree that **homosexual relations** between consenting adults should be legal?

38. What was the name given by the press to a giant eight-engined sea plane designed and built by **Howard Hughes** that made just one short flight in 1947?

39. Link these **college football team names** to the state: a) Wolverines b) Buckeyes c) Crimson Tide

40. Identify the state from the **state bird**: a) roadrunner b) cactus wren c) willow ptarmigan

41. The **bald eagle** may be an American symbol, but it had to be placed on the endangered species list in 1967. When was it removed from the list?

42. Which was most visited place in the **US National Park Service** system in 2015?

43. Mount Denali is the highest peak in America. Which is the **second highest**?

44. Navajo is the **most commonly spoken Native American language**, with about 169,000 speakers, according to the Census Bureau. Which language comes second?

45. How many people aged 5 and over who are living in America **speak Spanish** at home? (You can have 5 million either side.)

46. Where was the first **McDonald's** restaurant?

47. Athens, Georgia, has only 120,000 citizens but spawned **two well-known rock bands**. Who are they?

48. Where are the following **halls of fame**? a) rock and roll b) pro football c) national aviation

49. Bonnie and Clyde made headlines as a murderous duo of bank robbers at the height of the Great Depression. What were their surnames?

50. Thanksgiving is the biggest day for food consumption in the United States. What is the second biggest?

BENIGHTED KINGDOM
Britain

1. Which British monarch has **reigned the longest**?

2. How many people in the past 100 years have become **prime minister** without first having stood as party leader in a general election?

3. Since 1066, there have been **two English Kings** with a regnal title (eg Henry or George) that was not adopted by any of their successors. Name them.

4. What **proportion of the population of England and Wales is Muslim**? (You can have 2% either side.)

5. In which decade did Britain get its **first female MP**?

6. How many times has **London hosted the Olympic Games**?

 7. Only one politician has held all **four great offices of state**: home secretary, foreign secretary, chancellor of the exchequer and prime minister. Who?

8. What is the **highest rate of income tax** ever imposed in Britain and when?

9. In 2006 **Alexander Litvinenko**, a former KGB agent who fled to Britain, was poisoned with polonium while eating at a London restaurant. What kind of cuisine did it serve?

10. A "great paper-weight that for half a century sat upon men's minds, and when she was removed their ideas began to blow about all over the place haphazardly". Who was **H. G. Wells** describing?

11. Whose **friendly relations with the Nazis** were revealed in the Marburg files?

12. In 1976 Britain earned which **dubious economic honour**?

13. **Three territories**, while close to Britain, are governed as "crown dependencies" and are not part of the UK. Name any one of them.

14. "I count my blessings for the fact I don't have to go into **that pit**," remarked whom of what in 1991?

15. **Three British prime ministers** were born outside the country. Can you name two of them?

16. What do both the **largest and smallest constituencies** (by population) have in common?

17. Which **saintly figure** did Margaret Thatcher misquote outside 10 Downing Street after becoming prime minister in 1979?

18. Among Britain's prime ministers since the beginning of the 20th century, a) what is the most common **university** attended; and b) how many did not attend university?

19. To what did **Harold MacMillan** respond with the words, "Perhaps we could have a translation, I could not quite follow" in 1960?

20. Harold MacMillan's **"wind of change"** speech signalled the beginning of the end of the British Empire in which part of the world?

21. In what year was the **voting age** lowered to 18?

22. There are 282 "Munros" in Scotland. What is a **Munro**?

23. Who traditionally lived at **12 Downing Street**?

24. Of the four great offices of state, which has never been held by a **woman**?

25. What is the second most spoken **language** in Britain, according to the 2011 census?

26. To which British prime minister was President **John F. Kennedy** related by marriage?

27. Stephen Ward, a key figure in the **Profumo affair**—which ended in the resignation of John Profumo, a secretary of state for war under Harold MacMillan—was a member of which profession?

28. According to the book *All the Countries We've Ever Invaded*, how many of the 193 countries in the world have not experienced **a British military presence**? (You can have five either side.)

29. Only one British prime minister has been **assassinated**. Who?

30. Britain is often depicted as a crowded country. But what proportion of the **land area** has been built upon? (You can have 5% either side.)

31. The following were **nicknames** for which prime ministers? a) The Unknown Prime Minister b) Man of Peace c) The Coroner d) Dizzy e) Grey Man

32. In a career spanning half a century, what was **Winston Churchill's** first ministerial position and in what year was he appointed to it?

33. The word **Tory**, now a nickname for a member or supporter of the Conservative Party, originally meant what?

34. Which **country house** is traditionally given to the prime minister for weekend retreats?

35. As well as being the **first female mayor** and magistrate in Britain, Elizabeth Garrett Anderson was the first woman to qualify in which profession?

36. What were the **fishing disputes** between Britain and Iceland between the 1950s and 1970s known as?

37. Apart from their similar spelling and derivation, what links the names **Oliver and Olivia** in British culture?

38. Sake Dean Mahomet, a Muslim Indian soldier born in 1759, is credited with opening **Britain's first what**?

39. The first **UK-wide referendum** was held in what year and on what subject?

40. In 1915 Cecil Chubb was the last private owner of which **national landmark,** which he bought as a present for his wife?

41. Would you eat the following **British foods** as starter, main course or dessert? a) Mince pie b) Cullen skink c) Toad-in-the-hole

42. After Tony Blair's visit to Camp David in 2001, George W. Bush joked that they had taken the "**special relationship**" to a new level because he and the prime minister used the same brand of what?

43. Who married Margaret Kempson in 1942 and **Margaret Roberts** in 1951?

 44. Which city gets the **most average annual rainfall**: New Orleans, Orlando or London?

45. The **package of reforms** enacted on October 27, 1986, was known as what and revolutionised what?

46. Who was the last Briton to win a **Wimbledon singles title** before Andy Murray managed the trick in 2013?

47. Which **philosopher** most strongly influenced Enoch Powell, a Conservative politician known mostly for his anti-immigration stance and "rivers of blood" speech?

48. Since 1945 the three largest **parliamentary majorities** were won by which party leaders, in which years?

49. England's **national animal** is the lion. But what is Scotland's?

50. For what did Britain declare its support in the **Balfour Declaration** of 1917?

OCCIDENTS OF HISTORY
Europe

1. Europe is named after Europa, a figure from **Greek myth**. Which God abducted her, disguised as a bull?

2. Who, in Greek myth, was **Europa's son** and what is he most famous for?

3. Which planet has a **moon** called Europa?

4. The **signature** of which official appears on euro bank notes?

5. The word **euro** appears on notes in three alphabets. What are they?

6. Which country's euro **coins** feature the following? a) two flying swans b) the Birth of Venus c) a tree

7. Which European country is the **most unequal** according to the OECD? And which **the least**?

8. Which is the **most densely populated** country in Europe? And which the least?

9. How many **official languages** does the EU have (as of 2017)?

10. What **proportion of the EU population is Muslim**? (You can have 2% either side.)

11. How many European states (excluding the UK) have **hereditary monarchs**?

12. Name the **last emperors or kings** of: a) Austria-Hungary b) Italy c) Portugal d) Greece.

13. Who was **in charge of France** at the end of both the Second Republic and the Second Empire?

14. Which Europe-wide **competition** was watched by 182 million people in 2017?

15. Which EU country is most covered by **woodland**?

16. Which European country's **flag** has: a) a double-headed eagle b) the shape of the country itself c) a yellow sun on a red background?

17. **Charlemagne** is generally accepted as being the first Holy Roman Emperor; he was crowned by the Pope in 800 CE. But who was the last person to hold the title?

18. Which was the first European country to **give women the vote**? And which was **the last**?

19. According to the OECD in early 2017, which EU country had the **highest government spending** as a proportion of GDP?

20. And which EU country had the **lowest government spending** as a proportion of GDP?

21. The **EU institutions** have four presidents at any time. Which institutions do they lead?

22. Which **wars were ended** by: a) the Treaty of Utrecht b) the Congress of Vienna c) the Treaty of Frankfurt?

⚠ **23.** Put these French **monarchs called Charles** in chronological order: a) the Fat b) the Simple c) the Wise d) the Bald

24. Where are the current locations of these **historic states**? a) The Batavian Republic b) Alclud or Alt Clut c) The Helvetic Republic

25. Name the country where these **political parties** operate: a) Vlaams Belang b) Podemos c) Top 09 d) Democraten 66

26. How many independent states have emerged from the **former Yugoslavia**?

27. Britain had to invoke Article 50 of the Treaty of Lisbon in order to leave the EU. But what is the subject of **Article 49**?

28. As of 2017, which German Länder is **the largest by population**? And which is the **smallest**?

29. Which German Länder is **the largest by area**? And which is the **smallest**?

30. How many **cantons** are there in Switzerland?

31. What are the four official **languages of Switzerland**? And which fifth language is used on Swiss coins?

32. Which other European country uses the **Swiss franc** as its main currency?

33. Link these **Communist leaders** with the Eastern European countries they governed: a) Todor Zhivkov b) Gustáv Husák c) János Kádár

34. It is a running joke that it is impossible to **name three famous Belgians**. But what were these Belgians famous for? a) Leo Hendrik Baekeland b) Eddy Merckx c) Edda van Heemstra Hepburn-Ruston

35. Where are the following **European palaces** located? a) Sanssouci b) Nymphenburg c) Het Loo

36. There is no proof that **Adolf Hitler** and **Josef Stalin** ever met. But they did live in the same town in the same year. Where and when?

37. Can you tell which **quotes** are those of Hitler, and which of Stalin? a) "I believe in one thing only, the power of human will" b) "One death is a tragedy; one million is a statistic" c) "Death solves all problems—no man, no problem" d) "What good fortune for governments that the people do not think"

38. How many counties are there in the **Republic of Ireland**? And which are the largest and smallest by area?

39. Locate these **French wines** in the right region: a) Muscadet Sèvre et Maine b) Nuits-Saint-Georges c) Sauternes

⚠ **40.** The euro wasn't the first attempt to form a common European currency. Which four countries established the **Latin Monetary union** in 1865?

41. Which pairs of **European countries were united** from a) 1814 to 1905 b) 1815 to 1830 c) 1938 to 1945?

42. The Pope is historically associated with Rome. But in which city did **popes reside** from 1309 to 1377?

43. In which European cities are these **bridges**? a) Erasmus b) Chain c) Vasco da Gama

44. Which **Russian tsars:** a) emancipated the serfs b) defeated Napoleon c) started the Crimean war?

45. Which **court** was set up in 1959 and covers 47 countries, many of whom are not in the EU?

⚠ **46.** Which Eastern **European countries** saw failed rebellions against Communist rule in a) 1953 b) 1956 and c) 1968?

47. Three European countries were among the top five **most visited** by tourists in 2015, according to the UN World Tourism Organisation. Which were they?

48. In which EU countries, on the latest data, did citizens have the **longest life expectancy** at birth? And which two countries had the **shortest**?

49. Which **Roman emperor** a) was the last of the Claudian dynasty b) extended the empire to its greatest size c) was, according to one ancient historian, used as a footstool by the King of Persia?

50. Which European country was **partitioned** three times between 1772 and 1795, disappearing entirely in the process?

LATIN QUARTER
The Americas

1. What was the capital of the **Aztec empire**?

2. Money grew on trees in the Aztec and Mayan empires. What did they both use for **currency**?

3. What did the Aztecs use a **Tlachtli** for?

4. What did the **Treaty of Tordesillas** of 1494 decide?

5. One of the biggest prizes for the Spanish in South America was a **Bolivian mining town** situated 4,090 metres (13,419 ft) above sea level. What was its name and what did it produce?

6. How many countries in Latin America are considered Bolivarian, owing their independence in some way to **Simón Bolívar**?

7. Bernardo O'Higgins is an unlikely sounding South American leader. Of which country was he a **founding father**?

8. Peru enjoyed an economic boom from the mid-1840s to the mid-1860s thanks to **surging exports**. What was it exporting?

 9. The United States has not yet had a female president. How many times has macho Latin America elected **female presidents**?

10. Maximilian I was **emperor of Mexico** from 1864 to 1867. Which European leader placed him on the throne?

11. How long did Mexico's **Institutional Revolutionary Party** (PRI) hold power for in the 20th century without a break?

12. The **war of the triple alliance** between 1865 and 1870 was between Paraguay and which three nations?

13. The 1982 film *Missing*, starring Jack Lemmon, is about the disappearance of Charlie Horman, an American journalist, from which **country**?

14. Which was the last Latin American country to **abolish slavery** and when did it happen?

 15. Who started a colony in Paraguay for **anti-semitic Germans**?

16. In which city is the largest population of **people of Japanese descent** outside Japan found?

17. The **Amazon rainforest** spreads across nine countries. Which are they?

18. What proportion of the **world's oxygen** is produced by the Amazon rainforest? (You can have 2% either side.)

19. Everyone knows that the Amazon is the longest river in South America. But what is the **second longest**?

20. What is the **biggest lake** (by volume and surface area) in Latin America?

21. Which **body of water**, located in the North Atlantic to the northeast of the Caribbean, is the breeding ground for European eels?

22. In which country would you find the **Nazca Lines**?

23. Which is the **world's highest seat of government**?

24. What is **Mexico's largest province** by area?

25. How many **states** are there in Brazil?

26. Brazil's economy suffered from **hyperinflation** in the 1980s and 1990s. If something cost one *cruzeiro novo* in 1980, what would it cost in 1997?

27. From the 1950s to the 1980s, many Latin American countries followed an economic policy of **ISI**. What do the initials stand for?

28. What was **Project Cybersyn**, made up of hundreds of Telex machines linked together, designed to do in Salvador Allende's Chile?

29. Latin America had many **dictators** in the 20th century. Who ruled the longest?

30. Which Latin American country saw a "**dirty war**" from around 1976 to 1983?

31. The United States overthrew the government of Guatemala in 1954. Which **multinational** lobbied extensively for the action?

32. In 2016, the **FARC**, a guerrilla movement, finally agreed a peace deal with the Colombian government. But who founded it and when?

33. The **Shining Path** was a Maoist guerrilla movement in Peru. Who was its founder?

34. Which country in the Americas is **the least equal**, according to the World Bank? And which is **the most equal**?

35. Which states have the following **national birds**? a) Andean cock-of-the-rock b) resplendent quetzal c) doctor bird

36. How many **provinces** does Canada have? And which, by area, are the largest and smallest?

37. Which was the last Canadian province to **join the confederation**?

38. Match the **licence-plate slogan** to the Canadian province: a) Land of Living Skies b) Birthplace of Confederation c) Yours to Discover

39. Since 1930, when the tournament started, there have been 20 **football world cups**. How many have been won by Latin American countries?

40. The **Copa America** is the oldest international football competition. When did it start? And which country has won it the most times?

41. Football is Brazil's national sport. In which cities are the following **clubs** based? a) Palmeiras b) Corinthians c) Flamengo

42. The musical genre reggae was first developed in which **Caribbean country**?

43. The big nations tend to dominate the Olympic medal tables. But which **three Caribbean countries** won the most medals per capita at the 2016 Rio Olympics?

44. Diego Rivera was a Mexican mural painter. Which **equally famous painter** did he marry twice?

45. *Man at the Crossroads* was one of **Diego Rivera**'s most famous works. Why was it destroyed?

46. Which Argentinian author's collection of short stories of 1935, *A Universal History of Infamy*, is considered by some critics as the first work of the "**magical realist**" movement?

47. Which countries are these famous **Latin music stars** from? a) Rubén Blades b) Luis Miguel c) Juanes

48. From which countries do these **Latin dances** originate? a) cha-cha b) samba c) tango

49. Frank Sinatra sang that "there's an awful lot of coffee in Brazil" and the country has been the world's biggest producer for 150 years. But can you name the other four Latin American countries among the world's **top 10 coffee producers**?

50. Made with a mixture of cachaça (a spirit made from sugar cane), sugar and lime, what is the name of **Brazil's "national" cocktail**?

TO UR IS HUMAN
Middle East and Africa

1. What **proportion of the world's population lives in Africa**?

2. The Middle East produces about a third of the world's oil. Which is the **biggest producer** in the region?

3. The following **currencies** are used in which countries? a) cedi b) pula c) lilangeni d) dobra e) nakfa

4. Approximately **how many languages** are spoken throughout the continent of Africa?

 5. Over 360 tonnes of what are flown out of **Nairobi airport** every day?

6. **Sir Mark Sykes** and **François Georges-Picot** were appointed by which governments to do what when?

7. In which countries in the Middle East do **Shia Muslims make up a majority**?

8. What is the **meaning of the names** of the following groups? a) al Qaeda b) Ennahda c) Shabab

9. The **Kurds** are spread over which four countries?

10. Nkandla, a small village in KwaZulu-Natal in South Africa, is **notorious for what** reason?

11. Which city is known colloquially as **"the mother of the world"**?

12. In what year did these countries **gain their independence**? a) Algeria b) Uganda c) Burundi

13. Where did the **Arab Spring** begin?

 14. Which Middle Eastern government was **overthrown in 1953** and by whom?

15. According to the **National Pact**, an unwritten understanding dating back to 1943, the Lebanese president, prime minister and parliament's speaker must be drawn from which religious groups respectively?

16. In which city and in what year did the **peace accords** between the Israelis and Palestinians take place, then led by Yitzhak Rabin and Yasser Arafat?

17. Which African country is the **world's newest state**?

18. Who is the first and (as of 2017) only Arab to have won the **Nobel prize for literature**?

19. What is the significance of the **number 46664**?

20. In 2014 Nigeria became **Africa's largest economy** overnight. How?

21. Hosni Mubarak took over as president of Egypt in 1981 following what event?

22. Israel fought the the **six-day war** in 1967 with which Arab states?

23. In which decade and in which country was the **Muslim Brotherhood** founded?

24. Why are the cities of **Natanz** and **Fordow** of particular concern to Israel?

25. Which is the **largest country** (by geographic area) in the Arab world?

26. What is the world's **oldest seat of Muslim learning** and where is it located?

27. In what year was the **kingdom of Saudi Arabia** founded? a) 1901 b) 1911 c) 1929 d) 1932

28. At the end of the cold war, how many of Africa's 53 countries were **democracies**?

29. In October 2016, South Africa, the Gambia and Burundi announced their withdrawal from **which institution**, claiming it was biased against African states?

30. In 2008 **inflation in Zimbabwe** reached what rate (to the nearest million %)?

31. **Paul Biya** is the ruler of which country and has been since when? (You can have three years either side.)

32. The **borders of Lesotho** are notable for what reason?

33. Which document did the **African Union** launch in 2016 and who were the first two recipients?

34. In the **UN declaration of 1947**, was Jerusalem declared: a) the capital of Israel b) the capital of Palestine c) a joint capital or d) an international area under UN control?

35. On which **Jewish holiday** did an Arab coalition launch a war against Israel?

36. Only three countries in the world **recognised the Taliban** government in Afghanistan. Two were Arab. Which were they?

37. Which **Israeli politician** worked briefly with Mitt Romney at the Boston Consulting Group in 1976?

38. What proportion of the population of the Middle East is **aged between 15 and 29**? (You can have 5% either side.)

39. Which state owns **al-Jazeera**?

40. The following countries were run by which **colonial powers**: a) Rwanda b) the Democratic Republic of Congo c) Mozambique d) Nigeria?

41. The **son of which British prime minister** tried to orchestrate a coup in which African country in 2004?

42. Which African country **shares its name** with an Anglo-Saxon boy's name and the particles created when holes are punched in paper, such as on a voting ballot?

43. The **war between Iran and Iraq**, led by Ayatollah Khomeini and Saddam Hussein, lasted how long?

44. Which **prime minister** said: "In Israel, in order to be a realist you must believe in miracles"?

45. The **Rub al Khali desert** is also known as what?

46. Who was **Ethiopia's last emperor**?

47. King Faisal of Saudi Arabia was **murdered in 1975** by: a) his son b) his nephew or c) his butler?

48. What is notable about the **constitution of Israel**?

49. Which **French philosopher** did Ayatollah Ruhollah Khomeini meet while in exile in Paris?

50. **Africa** comprises what proportion of the world's land area? (You can have 2% either side.)

EAST SIDERS
Asia

1. The name of which central Asian republic's former capital city means **"father of apples"** in the local language?

2. The name of which south-east Asian city means **"lion city"** in Sanskrit?

3. Which south-east Asian capital city is known as **Krung Thep** by its inhabitants?

4. Located where the Klang and Gombak rivers meet, which south-east Asian capital city's name means **"muddy confluence"**?

5. Which country shifted its capital city to **Naypyidaw** in 2005?

6. In which Asian country has **gross national happiness**, rather than gross domestic product, been adopted as the measure of the nation's success?

7. By what name was **Bangladesh** known before it gained independence from Pakistan in 1971?

8. Which **waterway** connects the Andaman Sea and the South China Sea, running between the Indonesian island of Sumatra and Malaysia?

 9. Tsushima, a **naval battle that took place off the coast of Japan** in 1905, was fought between the forces of Japan and which country?

10. The flag of which Asian country is made up of **two overlapping triangles**?

11. The Yangtze is the **longest river** in Asia. Which rivers are second and third on the list?

12. Mount Everest is the **highest mountain** in Asia and the world at 29,000 feet. Which two are the next highest in Asia (and the world)?

13. Kisenosato became the **first Japanese person** in 19 years to do what in 2017?

14. Why should Japanese diners take care when eating **fugu**?

15. Tokyo is Japan's capital city. Which **two other cities** have been Japan's capital most recently?

16. Tokyo is hosting the **2020 Olympic Games**. When did Japan last stage an Olympic Games?

17. **Ikebana** is a Japanese art associated with what skill?

18. Seoul, the capital, is South Korea's largest city. Which is the **second largest**?

 19. How is **Saloth Sar**, who once ruled an Asian country, better known?

20. How many states are in the **Federated States of Micronesia**?

21. Put these languages of India in order of which has the **most native speakers**, starting with the largest: Telugu, Bengali, Hindi, Tamil, Marathi.

22. Which is India's **smallest state** by area?

23. Saparmurat Niyazov banned gold teeth, the circus and the opera because he disliked them and renamed the month of January after himself. Which central Asian country did the **mad despot** rule between 1985 and 2006?

24. Which central Asian country is **double landlocked**, that is, surrounded by countries that are themselves landlocked?

25. Dien Bien Phu was the decisive battle in which **20th-century war**?

26. Which **Vietnamese city**, the capital between 1802 and 1945, stands on the Perfume River?

27. What is the **currency** of Laos?

28. Which **Cambodian town** is closest to the temple complex of Angkor, the main tourist attraction in the country?

29. Jansher Khan, a Pakistani, was **world champion** at which sport for a record eight times?

30. India's film industry is known as Bollywood but by what -wood is **Pakistan's film industry** known?

31. Which **vast desert** covers most of the southern part of Mongolia?

32. From whom does the **Philippines** derive its name?

33. What **line of latitude** gives its name to the border between North and South Korea?

 34. Forming part of the border with China, what is the **longest river** in North Korea?

35. A museum in the northern Philippines city of Marikina houses a collection of what objects associated with **Imelda Marcos**, wife of Ferdinand Marcos, the country's ruler from 1965 to 1986, and first lady of the Philippines for 20 years?

36. Which **book by Alex Garland** tells the story of a group of young backpackers whose search for a supposedly idyllic Thai island ends in tragedy?

37. **Dr William Brydon** was the only survivor of an army slaughtered during an infamous British retreat from which Asian capital in 1842?

38. Which three Asian countries' borders meet at an area called the "**golden triangle**", known for its prodigious opium crop?

39. Where in Asia is the **least densely populated independent country** on the planet?

40. What species of **Asian rhino**, the most endangered large mammal on the planet, takes its name from the island where a tiny surviving wild population still clings on?

41. *Krakatoa: East of Java*, a disaster film made in 1969 starring Maximilian Schell, tells the story of the **volcanic eruption in 1883**. But Krakatoa is not east of Java. In which direction would you have to head to get there?

42. Which **breed of dog**, named after the island from which they are thought to originate, was designated a national monument by the South Korean government in 1962 to recognise its status as the country's national dog?

43. Which ruler born in 1336 close to Samarkand in present-day Uzbekistan claimed **Genghis Khan as a relation** and established a central Asian empire that stretched from India to Turkey?

44. The epitaph of which author, **buried in Samoa**, concludes with these lines from his poem, "Requiem": "Home is the sailor home from the sea, And the hunter home from the hill"?

45. A town and fishing port, a popular **tourist destination in Bangladesh**, is located on what is reputedly the world's longest beach, a stretch of sand 75 miles (121km) long, and is named after an officer of the British East India Company. What is it called?

46. What is the name of the **volcano** just 55 miles from Manila, capital of the Philippines, which erupted in 1991 after having lain dormant for 500 years? It was one of the most powerful eruptions of the 20th century.

47. Name the politician who successfully campaigned for an **independent Pakistan** and who became the country's first leader after independence in 1947.

48. The **Palk Strait** is located between which two Asian countries?

49. On its completion in 2004 the **101 Tower** was the world's tallest building. In which Asian capital is it to be found?

50. Which plant, whose name derives from the Greek words for rose tree, is the **national flower** of Nepal?

DRAGON'S DEN
China

1. How many stars are on the **Chinese flag**?

2. Russia has nine **time zones** and the continental United States has four. How many time zones are there in China?

3. **Confucius**, the noted Chinese philosopher and political theorist, was born in which century?

4. Name the **military treatise** attributed to Sun Tzu and written in around the fifth century BCE that is still read today for its insights into winning in battle as well as in business.

5. The "**Four Great Ancient Capitals of China**" is a recognised collection of cities that have served as the country's capitals down the ages. Beijing is one; can you name any others?

6. Farmers digging a well in 1974 close to Xian, capital of Shaanxi province, made what **archaeological discovery** that is now a major tourist attraction?

7. Whose **dying words** were reputedly "I have not told half of what I saw" in reference to his extensive travels in China?

8. What are **Hakka, Wu, Min, Xiang** and **Gan**?

9. What is the name of the **complex of religious buildings** located in the Chongwen district of Beijing and first completed in 1420 by a Ming emperor, Yongle, though since enlarged and rebuilt?

10. Zheng He, the great Chinese admiral, embarked on seven voyages between 1405 and 1433. What was the **furthest point** he reached?

11. Located on the west side of Tiananmen Square in Beijing and opened in 1958, what building is the venue for the **National People's Congress**, state banquets and many other important state events?

12. A palace in Lhasa, capital of Tibet, was once the **winter home of the Dalai Lama**. What is it called?

13. **Kunming Lake**, a peaceful and scenic spot close to the centre of Beijing, is a central feature of which tourist attraction?

14. The **Grand Canal**, a vast waterway system over 1,100 miles in length, stretches from Beijing to which city on China's eastern seaboard?

15. The Three Gorges dam, opened in 2008, spans which **large Chinese river**?

16. What name is given to the **war** between China and invading British and French forces that culminated in the looting and destruction of the Summer Palace in Beijing in 1860?

17. **Fragrant Harbour** is a translation of the name of what part of China?

18. What was the name of the **uprising** during which a rebel force hoping to establish a "Heavenly Kingdom of Great Harmony" attempted to overthrow the ruling Manchu dynasty between 1850 and 1864?

19. By what name is an uprising in 1900 against western influence in China led by a clandestine organisation known as the **Society of the Righteous and Harmonious Fists** better known?

20. **Pu Yi**, the last emperor of China, was deposed in 1911. But where was he made emperor later in his life?

21. By what name is the **nationalist party** that ruled China between 1928 and 1949 usually known?

22. What "incident" was used by Japan as a **pretext for invading China** in 1937, the start of the second Sino-Japanese war?

23. **Mao Zedong** was born in which province of China?

24. Why did Mao ask Chinese citizens to **bang pots and pans** during the Great Leap Forward?

25. **Jiang Qing, Zhang Chunqiao, Yao Wenyuan,** and **Wang Hongwen** were known collectively by what name?

26. The Taiping rebellion convulsed China from 1850 to 1864. Who did its leader, **Hong Xiuquan**, claim to be?

27. **Hong Kong** was handed back to the Chinese in 1997 under an agreement that it would be treated differently from the rest of the nation—"one country, two systems". When will the arrangement end?

28. Which **tropical island** is both the smallest and southernmost of China's provinces?

29. Hohhot is the capital of which **autonomous region of China**?

30. What is the name of the **desert in Xinjiang province** that is the largest in China?

31. China's longest land border is with Mongolia at 2,900 miles (4,667km). Hong Kong and Macau aside, with which country does it have its **shortest land border**?

32. In which of China's main cities is **Pudong**, the financial and business district?

33. Which large city in southern China is also known as the "**City of Five Rams**"?

34. After Beijing and Shanghai, which **southern city** is China's third largest by population?

35. What is the name of the remote site between the Takla Makan and Kumtag deserts that is the country's only **nuclear weapons test facility**?

36. What **ethnic group**, roughly 12 million strong and mostly Muslim, live in Xinjiang, a province in China's far west?

37. What is the more common name of the **Chinese lion dog**, a toy breed considered the exclusive property of the royal court during the Ming and Manchu dynasties?

38. Two breeds of dog that originated in China have **blue tongues**. Can you name either or both?

39. The **giant panda** is China's most famous animal, often used as a diplomatic gift. Which American leader received Ling-Ling and Hsing-Hsing, star attractions at Washington zoo?

 40. What are employed in an unusual **traditional fishing method** in use for over 1,000 years on the Li River in Guilin province?

41. What is the main ingredient of **har gau dumplings**, a popular variety of dim sum, the small plates of steamed baskets of bite-sized food originating in southern China?

42. What controversial **delicacy** is the centrepiece of a 10-day festival held in the southern city of Yulin every July to coincide with the summer solstice?

43. Why is **gunpowder tea**, a variety of the Chinese beverage, so called?

44. Baijiu, a strong and powerfully flavoured Chinese **alcoholic drink**, is generally distilled from what grain?

45. What is the name of the Chinese **ride-hailing app**, which bought Uber's Chinese unit in 2016 and claims 400 million users across 400 cities?

46. Not astronauts or cosmonauts, by what name have **Chinese who travel into space** been christened by the western media?

47. What links **Yanbian Funde, Liaoning Whowin, Beijing Sinobo Guoan** and **Guangzhou Evergrande Taobao**?

48. Name the **conceptual artist** born in 1957 whose works include filling the turbine hall at Tate Modern in London with millions of porcelain sunflower seeds in 2010.

49. Which **film** directed by Zhang Yimou, a surprise hit with western audiences after its release in 1991, tells the story of the fourth wife of a rich and ageing clan leader?

50. Which **play** about a divorced couple, both recently remarried, who accidentally book adjoining suites at the same hotel for their honeymoons, was completed by Noel Coward during a stay at Shanghai's Peace Hotel (then known as the Cathay Hotel) in 1930?

NATIONAL INQUIRERS
International

1. Rank these countries by the **number of guns** for every 100 residents, from highest to lowest: Switzerland, New Zealand, Germany, United States, Russia, Iraq.

2. In how many countries are **same-sex relationships** outlawed (to the nearest five)?

3. How many countries are members of the **Universal Postal Union**, the United Nations agency that coordinates postal policies between states and internationally?

 4. The Synchrotron-light for Experimental Science and Applications in the Middle East, or Sesame, is a notable **scientific enterprise** because of the countries involved; name at least six of them.

5. The members of which faith have, on average, the highest number of **years of schooling**?

6. Which is the world's **fastest growing religion** and what is its projected growth between 2015 and 2060?

7. There are two non-member permanent **observer states** at the United Nations; which are they?

8. In 2015 and 2016 what were the three most common countries of origin for those **seeking asylum** for the first time in Europe?

9. Which of the following countries is not a member of the **North Atlantic Treaty Organization**: France, Sweden, Norway, Iceland, Turkey?

10. The **Hague Convention** covers what?

11. How many people in the world are in **prison**, to the nearest million?

12. In 2013, the most recent year for which reliable data exists, what proportion of the world's population was officially **deemed to be poor** (to the nearest 3%)?

13. In which five countries or regions are the United Nations' largest **peacekeeping missions** stationed?

14. Since its creation in 2002, how many detainees have been brought to the **Guantanamo Bay** detention camp (to the nearest 25)?

15. Name five countries in which **voting** is compulsory.

16. Approximately what proportion of pregnancies worldwide end in **abortion**?

17. Since its establishment in 1945, the United Nations has had nine **secretary-generals**. Name at least five and where they came from.

18. Put these countries in order, from highest to lowest, for their **marriage rates**: Switzerland, Japan, Italy, China, Russia, Britain.

19. The signatories to the **Paris accord** have agreed to limit the increase in the global average temperature to what?

20. In which of these countries does the **foreign-born population** make up more or less than 10% of the total: Sweden, America, Britain, Russia, France? Is the proportion growing or shrinking?

21. How many **mountains** around the world soar above 8,000 metres (26,247ft)?

22. In 21 countries, including Nigeria, India, Bangladesh and Pakistan, the **national minimum age of criminal responsibility** is the lowest in the world. What is it?

23. Which is the **cheapest citizenship** you can buy?

24. In which years were the following **international organisations** founded: a) the United Nations b) the World Health Organization c) the World Trade Organization?

25. Which of the following countries is NOT a member of **OPEC**, an intergovernmental organization with 14 members that was founded in Baghdad in 1960: a) Qatar b) Algeria c) Brazil d) Venezuela e) Iraq?

26. The **International Criminal Court** has faced criticism because the 39 individuals indicted in the first 15 years of its existence all have one thing in common. What?

27. What proportion of the world's adults **smoke**?

28. What was the significance of **United Nations Resolution 1441**?

⚠ **29.** Between 1966 and 2016, what proportion of countries in the world at some point had a **female head of state** or government (excluding monarchs) for at least a year?

30. Among members of the OECD, a group of rich countries, which offers the most generous **maternity leave**?

31. In 1960 **Fidel Castro** spent 4 hours and 29 minutes setting a world record—for what?

32. **Smallpox** is the only infectious disease ever to have been eradicated. In what year was this officially declared?

33. Which three countries have the highest **murder rates** in the world (as a proportion of the population)?

34. Of the million most visited websites, what percentage is dedicated to **pornography** (answers within 5 percentage points)?

35. What proportion of the world's population lives in **cities**?

36. What is notable about more than **half of all births** in Brazil, the Dominican Republic and Egypt?

37. In which cities do the following **organisations** have their headquarters: a) the United Nations b) the International Criminal Court c) International Energy Agency d) the International Pacific Halibut Commission?

38. Around a third of countries now meet the International Labour Organisation's standards on maternity leave (at least 14 weeks off for new mothers, paid at two-thirds their salary and funded publicly). What proportion meets the IlO's standards for **paternity leave**?

39. What is the United Nations' **foreign aid target** for donor countries?

40. Which cities hosted the summer **Olympics** in the following years: a) 1896 b) 1936 c) 1972 d) 1992?

41. The most destructive **eruption** on earth in the past 500 years happened in which century and in which country?

42. What proportion of countries has laws or policies penalising **blasphemy**?

43. World **life expectancy** is currently what? Which country's citizens have the longest life expectancy and which have the shortest?

44. The **Nobel Peace Prize** has on two occasions been shared by three people. Name either trio.

45. Which was the first country to offer **e-residency**?

46. Which three countries boast the most **meth labs** (as calculated by the number of labs shut down by their governments)?

47. Which country is thought to have **broadcast the first debates** between candidates vying to be the head of government?

48. What does the **Doomsday Clock** measure?

49. In 2014 the **World Health Organization** held its first summit on ending what?

50. Which continent is the **least safe** for road users?

FIRM FAVOURITES
Business

1. The original logo of which company, founded in 1976, featured a picture of **Isaac Newton** sitting under a tree?

2. The badge of which **Japanese car company** features a representation of the star cluster known as Pleiades or the Seven Sisters?

3. And which Japanese car company takes its name from a **Zoroastrian god**?

4. Which two sports brands were the result of a bitter falling out between the **Dassler brothers** in Germany in the 1940s?

5. Which technology company was initially called **BackRub** before adopting a much better known corporate identity?

6. What objects prompted **Marcus Samuel** to expand his business as an antique dealer in London in the 1830s to import them? They gave rise to a different business which still bears their name today.

7. Which company had the advertising slogan "**Think Different**"?

8. And which company had the slogan "**A Diamond is Forever**"?

9. And whose slogan was "**Fly the Friendly Skies**"?

10. Which company's slogan was "**Have It Your Way**"?

11. And who had the slogan "**Think Small**"?

12. Which company used the slogan "**We Try Harder**"?

13. What do the initials in the name **J. C. Penney** stand for?

14. And what about the initials in **F. W. Woolworth**?

15. What do the initials stand for in **L. L. Bean**?

16. How did **A&M** records get its name?

17. How did **JCB** get its name?

18. What does **IKEA** stand for?

19. **M&Ms** are a popular snack. What do the initials stand for?

20. What does **LVMH** stand for?

21. Which company shares its name with a race of legendary beings in *Gulliver's Travels*?

22. What do the initials stand for in **IBM**?

23. What does **BMW** stand for?

24. What do the initials in **FIAT** stand for?

25. What do the Ms stand for in **3M**?

26. And what do the initials stand for in **LG** electronics?

27. Which **Formula 1 motor racing world champion** quit the sport in 1979 to run the airline he established the same year?

28. The logo of **Chupa Chups**, a popular brand of lollypop, was designed by which well-known artist?

29. **Patrick Bateman**, anti-hero of the novel *American Psycho* by Bret Easton Ellis, worked for which fictional Wall Street investment firm?

30. **George Clooney** plays Ryan Bingham of the Career Transitions Corporation, firing people for a living on behalf of firms laying off staff, in which film?

⚠ **31.** In the film *Blade Runner*, Ridley Scott's dystopian vision of the future, what is the name of the **powerful high-tech firm** responsible for building replicates, including (spoiler alert) Harrison Ford's character, Deckard?

32. In which film does a piece of technology deliver this line: "**I am a HAL 9000 computer.** I became operational at the H.A.L. plant in Urbana, Illinois, on the 12th of January 1992"?

33. What **fictional airline** is used in several films, TV programmes and books which feature plane crashes or other aviation disasters, including *Lost*, *Executive Decision*, *Diagnosis Murder* and the *X-Files*?

34. Britain's **first purpose-built international airport** was located in which suburb of London?

35. Until the construction of Orly in 1932, which was **Paris's only international airport**? It is still in use today.

36. Which **American artist** summed up his approach to his work with this quote: "Making money is art and working is art and good business is the best art"?

37. Which **American president** said "the chief business of the American people is business"?

38. Which hugely **successful American investor** remarked: "In the business world, the rearview mirror is always clearer than the windshield"?

39. Which **British statesman** said: "Some people regard private enterprise as a predatory tiger to be shot. Others look on it as a cow they can milk. Not enough people see it as a healthy horse, pulling a sturdy wagon"?

40. Which country is the world's biggest producer of **natural gas**?

41. Which country was the world's biggest producer of **crude oil** in 2016?

42. Which country is the world's biggest **coal** producer?

43. Which country's residents are the biggest **beer drinkers** per head of population?

44. Which **French firm** is the world's biggest-selling cosmetics business?

45. What is the name of the **media conglomerate** that counts NBC, Universal Pictures, Working Title Films and GolfNow among its subsidiaries?

46. Which **tech company** was formed by Gordon Moore and Robert Noyce?

47. Which company did Larry **Page** and Sergey **Brin** found?

48. Which company was founded by **Jack Ma**?

49. Travis **Kalanick** and Garrett **Camp** founded which company?

50. Jeff Bezos founded Amazon in 1995. But which **newspaper** did he buy in 2013?

CAPITAL BRAINS
Finance and economics

1. From what **language** does the word economics derive?

2. Who coined the term **"dismal science"** to describe economics?

3. The award known as the **Nobel prize for economics** was first presented in 1969. What occasion prompted the creation of the prize?

4. Who was the **first woman** to be awarded the economics prize and when did this happen?

5. **John Maynard Keynes** didn't get a degree in economics. What did he study as an undergraduate?

6. Link the **quotes** to the economists: a) "Capitalism is the astounding belief that the most wickedest of men will do the most wickedest of things for the greatest good of everyone" b) "Most economic fallacies derive from the tendency to assume that there is a fixed pie, that one party can gain only at the expense of another" c) "Open immigration can't exist with a strong social safety net; if you're going to assure health care and a decent income to everyone, you can't make that offer global" d) "Economics has never been a science—and it is even less now than a few years ago"

7. Where does the term **"priming the pump"** come from, as an economic adage?

8. Which people are associated with the following economic **"laws"**? a) bad money drives out good b) supply creates its own demand c) when a measure becomes a target, it ceases to be a good measure

9. What do these economic **initials** stand for? a) PPP b) FDI c) PMI

10. Which economists came up with the following **concepts**? a) the theory of comparative advantage b) countries will export products that use their abundant and cheap factors of production and import products that use their scarce factors c) theory of marginal utility

11. **Daniel Kahneman** won the Nobel prize in economics in 2002. But his academic background was not in economics. What was it?

12. Which economics professor had a cameo in the movie *The Big Short*, alongside Selena Gomez?

13. Which **British economist**, who died in 2010, devoted much of his work to establishing data on economic growth through history?

14. What do these **acronyms** stand for? a) EBITDA b) CAPE c) RMBS

15. Which **countries**, based on the World Bank report for 2015, had: a) the highest GDP per capita b) the lowest GDP per capita?

16. Which countries, based on the latest World Bank data, were: a) the **most unequal** and b) the **least**?

17. What proportion of **US mutual funds** investing in large-company shares outperformed their benchmark over the 15 years to end 2016, according to Standard & Poor's? What about funds investing in small-company shares? (You can have 5% either side.)

18. What do the **initials** stand for in the following? a) JP Morgan b) ING c) BBVA

 19. Which **famous financier** travelled under the pseudonym of Professor Clarence Skinner?

20. Which **chairmen of the Federal Reserve** said the following? a) "I guess I should warn you, if I turn out to be particularly clear, you've probably misunderstood what I've said" b) "The Federal Reserve, as one writer put it, is in the position of the chaperone who has ordered the punch bowl removed just when the party was really warming up" c) "The only useful thing banks have invented in 20 years is the ATM"

21. Which chairmen of the Federal Reserve had the following **characteristics**? a) a disciple of Ayn Rand who played the clarinet b) a cigar smoker who was 6ft 7in (2.01 metres) tall c) a president of the New York Stock Exchange at 31, dubbed "the boy wonder of Wall Street"

22. The book ***Barbarians at the Gate*** is about the takeover of which firm?

23. Warren Buffett, who runs the conglomerate Berkshire Hathaway, is often regarded as the greatest investor of all time. But who was his **investment guru**?

24. What **branch of finance** is associated with head-and-shoulders patterns, Japanese candlesticks or Fibonacci numbers?

25. The Bank of England introduced **new polymer £5 notes** featuring a portrait of Winston Churchill in November 2016, but why did some individuals and organisations refuse to take the note?

26. Link the **slogan** to the financial services firm or brand: a) One client at a time b) It's everywhere you want to be c) Don't leave home without it

27. The post–second world war exchange rate system is often called the **Bretton Woods** system after a conference that agreed it. Where is Bretton Woods?

28. Who led the **British and American delegations** at Bretton Woods?

29. At Bretton Woods, the assembled countries agreed to set up **two multinational institutions**. What were they?

30. During the operation of Bretton Woods, economists Robert Mundell and Marcus Fleming came up with the idea of a **trilemma**, or impossible trinity, to explain the limits of currency systems. What are the three elements of the trilemma?

31. By an informal arrangement, the **head of the World Bank** has always come from which country?

32. Five out of the eleven **directors-general** of the International Monetary Fund have come from which nation?

33. Which countries have the following **stock market indices**? a) Sensex b) Ibex c) Kospi d) Bovespa

34. Which countries have the following **currencies**? a) togrog b) dong c) lempira d) guarani

35. Which civilisations had the following **coins**? a) solidus b) auksinas c) owl

 36. What proportion of US dollars in circulation is in the form of **$100 bills**? (You can have 5% either side.)

37. What are the full names of these **bank divisions**? a) ECM b) DCM c) FICC

38. The Bank for International Settlements is often described as the "**central bankers' central bank**". Where is it based?

39. The **World Trade Organization** sets the rules for global trade and had 164 member countries at the time of writing. But in what year was it set up and where is it based?

40. What are **contango** and **backwardation**?

41. The **Dodd-Frank Act** was the attempt to reform America's financial system after the credit crisis. In terms of pages, how long was it? (You can have 50 pages either side.)

42. By contrast, how many pages was the **Glass-Steagall Act**, passed during the Depression, that separated commercial and investment banking? (You can have five pages either side.)

43. In his bestselling economics book *Capital in the 21st Century*, Thomas Piketty linked rising inequality to the **equation $r > g$**. What do the letters stand for?

44. Which authors wrote the following **classic financial books**? a) *Reminiscences of a Stock Operator* b) *Manias, Panics and Crashes* c) *Where Are the Customers' Yachts?*

45. **Walter Bagehot** was one of the first editors of *The Economist*. But what was the title of his book, still cited as a guideline for central banks facing financial crises?

46. Some investors like to buy the bonds of riskier companies known as **speculative or junk bonds,** because they offer higher yields. The top credit rating from Standard & Poor's is AAA and from Moody's AA1. At what level do bonds start getting rated as junk?

47. Fraudulent investment plans are named **Ponzi schemes** after Charles Ponzi, who operated in the early 1920s. What did he claim was the source of his profits (he promised to double investors' money within 90 days)?

48. Many thriller plots have been based on an investment product called a **tontine**. How does it work?

49. Which **two winners** of the Nobel economics prize were directors of the failed hedge fund, Long-Term Capital Management?

50. Which **financial collapses** were the subjects of the following books?
a) *When Genius Failed* b) *The Smartest Guys in the Room* c) *House of Cards*

TURING TEST
Science and technology

1. Which **chemical element** has the shortest name?

2. Which chemical element has the **longest** name?

3. Four elements are named after the same **village in Sweden**. Which are they, and what is the name of the village?

 4. How many elements are gases at **room temperature** and pressure?

5. "O be a fine girl, kiss me" is a **mnemonic** for what?

6. Which **astronomical object** was discovered on January 1st 1801?

7. What links **M1** and **1054**?

8. Which gas makes up **1% of air**?

9. Which **five letters** convert RNA into DNA?

10. On which group of **crustaceans** was Charles Darwin acknowledged as the world's expert?

11. What **colour** is water?

12. What can be **up or down**, have charm, be strange or be either top or bottom?

13. Where in the human body would you find a pair of **sea horses**?

14. Where are the **Islets of Langerhans**?

15. Who wrote the following, and in what context: "It has not escaped our notice that the specific pairing we have postulated immediately suggests a possible **copying mechanism** for the genetic material"?

16. What distinguishes a **eukaryotic cell** from a prokaryotic one?

17. If talc=1, calcite=3, apatite=5 and quartz=7, **what equals 9**?

18. In which **constellation** is the middle of the Milky Way galaxy?

19. What is the most distant object in the universe discovered before the **invention of telescopes**?

20. After what are the **Ordovician** and **Silurian** geological periods named?

21. How old is the **Earth**?

22. How old is the **universe**?

23. Where would you find a **Golgi apparatus**?

24. What did the **Michelson-Morley experiment** show?

25. In which **geological period** did the dinosaurs depicted in the movie *Jurassic Park* live?

26. In 1905 **Albert Einstein** published four scientific papers. Two were on the theory of relativity and one on quantum theory. What was the other about?

27. To a chemist, what do the letters **s, p, d** and **f** have in common?

 28. What is **PSR B1257+12**, and why is it historically significant?

29. How many carbon atoms are there in a **buckyball** (a molecule of buckminsterfullerene)?

30. After hydrogen and helium, what is the **most common element** in the universe?

31. Where is the **Heaviside layer**?

32. What does the "**disposable soma**" theory purport to explain?

33. What was the name of the **first spacecraft** to make a soft landing on a planet other than Earth?

34. Which of the sun's eight planets has the most **eccentric orbit**?

 35. What links **geese, honeybees** and **sticklebacks**?

36. Besides the Galapagos Islands, where is it still possible to find **wild giant tortoises**?

37. What is made by the **Haber process**?

38. What starts life in the **Oort cloud**?

39. To an astronomer, what are the **Greeks** and the **Trojans**?

40. What distinguishes a **Gram-positive bacterium** from a **Gram-negative** one?

41. **Marie Curie** discovered radium and which other chemical element?

42. What can be **Batesian, Mullerian** or **Vavilovian**?

43. What is a **tektite**?

44. What is a **syncytium**?

45. What is **"trans"** in a trans fat?

46. What does the **Drake equation** attempt to describe?

47. The **Monument to the Great Fire of London** was also intended to be a scientific instrument. What sort?

48. What is a **Calvin cycle**?

49. Which year is defined as "the present" for the purpose of **calculating ages** as "years before present", or "BP"?

50. Who is supposed to have said, "I do not know what I may appear to the world, but to myself I seem to have been only like a boy playing on the seashore, and diverting myself in now and then finding a smoother pebble or a prettier shell than ordinary, whilst the **great ocean of truth** lay all undiscovered before me"?

LITERARY DEVICES
Books and arts

1. What were the talents of these **Greek muses**? a) Terpsichore b) Urania
   c) Clio

2. Identify the books and **female authors** from these four opening sentences:
   a) The old woman remembered a swan she had bought many years ago in
   Shanghai for a foolish sum. b) The snow in the mountains was melting
   and Bunny had been dead for several weeks before we came to understand
   the gravity of our situation. c) You better not never tell nobody but God.
   It'd kill your Mammy. d) Imagine a ruin so strange it must never have
   happened. First picture the forest. I want you to be its conscience, the eyes
   in the trees.

3. Identify the books and the **male authors** from these opening lines: a) Six
   North Africans were playing boule beneath Flaubert's statue. b) Beyond
   the Indian hamlet, upon a forlorn strand, I happened on a trail of recent
   footprints. c) This is a true story but I can't believe it's really happening.
   It's a murder story too. I can't believe my luck. d) Excuse me, sir, but may I
   be of assistance? Ah, I see I have alarmed you. Do not be frightened by my
   beard; I am a lover of America.

 4. Which famous authors have written under the following **pen-names**?
   a) Mary Westmacott b) Alice Addertongue c) Clive Hamilton
   d) Acton Bell

5. How are these **painters** better known? a) Domenikos Theotokopoulos b) Michelangelo Merisi c) Moishe Shagal d) Donato di Niccolò di Betto Bardi

6. Name these **winners of the Nobel prize for literature** based on the language used in their citation: a) for works of lyrical beauty and ethical depth, which exalt everyday miracles and the living past, b) who emulates the jesters of the Middle Ages in scourging authority and upholding the dignity of the downtrodden, c) that epicist of the female experience, who with scepticism, fire and visionary power has subjected a divided civilisation to scrutiny, d) for a poetic oeuvre of great luminosity, sustained by a historical vision, the outcome of a multicultural commitment.

7. Name the authors of these novels, generally agreed to be **post-modernist**: a) *You Shall Know Our Velocity* b) *1Q84* c) *Infinite Jest* d) *Inherent Vice*

8. Name the authors who invented these **fictional action heroes**: a) Myron Bolitar b) Jack Reacher c) Alex Cross d) Harry Bosch

9. Scandi noir is a popular genre of thrillers. But from which **Scandinavian country** did the following TV series originate? a) *Modus* b) *Acquitted* c) *The Killing*

10. And which **Scandinavian writers** feature the following detectives? a) Harry Hole b) Kurt Wallander c) Konrad Sejer

11. The following titles have won the **Pulitzer Prize** for biography since 2000. But who were the subjects of the books? a) *The First Tycoon* b) *American Lion* c) *American Prometheus*

12. Which thinkers wrote the following **influential books**? a) *A Theory of Justice* b) *The End of History and the Last Man* c) *Orientalism*

13. Which genres are the focus of the following **literary awards**? a) The Newbery Medal b) The Hugo Award c) Ruth Lilly prize.

14. The **Prix Goncourt** is France's premier literary prize. But which of the following never won? a) Simone de Beauvoir b) Marcel Proust c) Albert Camus d) Michel Houellebecq

15. Which authors set their works in the following **fictional counties**? a) Yoknapatawpha b) Maycomb c) Barsetshire

16. What do the **initials** stand for in these authors' names? a) e e cummings b) V. S. Naipaul c) A. S. Byatt d) T. S. Eliot

17. Excluding religious and propaganda texts, what is the **bestselling book of all time**?

18. Where are the following **ancient documents** currently housed? a) The Mappa Mundi b) The Dead Sea Scrolls and c) The Book of Kells

19. Which works of art or artists received the following **rejection letters**? a) The girl doesn't, it seems to me, have a special perception or feeling which would lift that book above the 'curiosity' level. b) Guitar groups are on their way out. c) An absurd and uninteresting fantasy which was rubbish and dull. d) I rack my brains why a chap should need thirty pages to describe how he turns over in bed before going to sleep.

20. Many countries change the titles of **Hollywood movies** to appeal to domestic audiences. The following are literal translations of four such film titles. What were their original Hollywood names? a) *The Night of the Cold Noses* b) *The Rebel Novice* c) *He's a Ghost!* d) *The Young People who Traverse Dimensions Wearing Sunglasses*

⚠ **21.** The **Golden Raspberry** awards or Razzies are awarded for the worst films or performances each year. Which actor and actress have received the most awards?

22. Film directors are usually more famous than their cinematographers. But which **cinematographers** are linked to the following movies? a) *The Shining* b) *The Seventh Seal* c) *Citizen Kane*

23. The Academy Award for best foreign-language film was first handed out in 1956. As of 2017, which country had **received the most awards**?

24. The Indian film industry is called Bollywood. But where is **Nollywood** based?

25. If you adjust for inflation, what was the **highest-grossing film** of all time?

26. Six degrees of **Kevin Bacon** is a popular game for movie buffs, in which any actor can be linked to the Hollywood star via joint film appearances. But which of these six films did Mr Bacon NOT appear in? a) *Wild Things* b) *The River Wild* c) *Mystic River* d) *A Few Good Men* e) *Twister* f) *JFK*

27. *Pride and Prejudice* is Jane Austen's most popular book and has been adapted for TV and film many times. But who played **Elizabeth Bennet** to the following Mr Darcys? a) Laurence Olivier b) Matthew Macfadyen c) Colin Firth

28. In which 2001 film did **Colin Firth** play a different character called Darcy?

29. Which **novels** were the following movies based on? a) *Apocalypse Now* b) *Tamara Drewe* c) *Clueless*

30. The following US shows were **spin-offs** from which original TV programmes? a) *Frasier* b) *Better Call Saul* c) *Melrose Place*

31. These British TV shows were adapted for the American market. What were their **US titles**? a) *Steptoe and Son* b) *Till Death Us Do Part* c) *Man About the House*

32. In which **galleries** would you find these artworks? a) *Venus de Milo* b) *The Three Graces* by Rubens c) *The Birth of Venus* by Botticelli d) *The Night Watch* by Rembrandt

33. The **Turner prize** is an award given to avant-garde artists. But in what media did the following artists work? a) Laure Prouvost b) Richard Wright c) Grayson Perry

34. **George Balanchine** is regarded as one of the greatest American choreographers, co-founding the New York City Ballet. Where was he born?

35. Pablo Picasso's works are often divided into **different periods**. Which came first—the Rose period, the Blue period or Cubism?

36. Which artists painted the following works? a) *Bedroom in Arles* b) *Le bonheur de vivre* c) *The Card Players*

37. Which **artists** were the (main) subjects of the following movies? a) *Girl with a Pearl Earring* b) *The Agony and the Ecstasy* c) *Lust for Life*

38. Which **sculptors** are responsible for the following works? a) *Lobster Trap and Fish Tail* b) *Bicycle Wheel* c) *Nuclear Energy*

39. Which **architects** designed the following buildings? a) the Pompidou Centre b) the Guggenheim Museum in Bilbao c) Guangzhou Opera House

40. Which **architectural styles** do these buildings represent? a) The Catherine Palace in Tsarskoye Selo b) The Château de Maisons in Maisons-Laffitte c) Chartres Cathedral

41. New York's theatre prizes are known informally as the **Tony awards**. What is the official title?

42. Which **types of music** are covered by the following awards? a) GMA Dove b) Mobo c) Lo Nuestro

43. In which **Shakespeare plays** do the following female characters appear? a) Hippolyta b) Isabella c) Hermione

44. Which Shakespeare plays feature the following **male characters**? a) Enobarbus b) Feste c) Orlando

45. On which Shakespeare plays were the following **musicals or films** based? a) *Throne of Blood* b) *Kiss Me Kate* c) *She's the Man*

46. Which **writing teams** were responsible for these famous musicals? a) *Oklahoma* b) *Chicago* c) *West Side Story*

47. From which **operas** do the following arias come? a) Largo al factótum b) La donna e mobile c) Che gelida manina

48. Name the **rock songs** that feature these lyrics, all of which mention US presidents: a) "Harry Truman, Doris Day, Red China, Johnnie Ray" b) "Do you remember your President Nixon, do you remember the bills you have to pay?" c) "We talk about Reaganomics, Oh Lord, down in the Congress"

49. *Billboard* has been producing a top albums chart for America every week since 1956. Which album spent the **most weeks at number 1** on the list?

50. Which **album** spent the **most weeks on the *Billboard* chart**? And which group had the **most top 10 albums**?

THE ANSWERS

MENTAL STATES: US

1. **Fifty-six**, although they didn't all sign on the same date. One of those who signed, Richard Stockton, later recanted. Eight of the signatories were born in Britain. Twenty-six copies survive; one was found in the back of a painting bought at a Philadelphia flea market in 1989. The painting cost $4; the declaration was eventually sold for $8.1 million in 2000.

2. **Fourteen**. The flag was sewn by Mary Pickersgill, born appropriately in 1776, her daughter, two nieces and an indentured servant. The song was written after Fort McHenry in Baltimore survived a British bombardment.

3. **Bacon's rebellion**. The dissidents, led by Nathaniel Bacon, were rebelling against the rule of Sir William Berkeley, governor of Virginia. The settlers wanted a harsher policy against Native Americans.

4. **Five**. John Quincy Adams (1824), Rutherford B. Hayes (1876), Benjamin Harrison (1888), George W. Bush (2000) and Donald Trump (2016). Victory is dependent not on the popular vote, but on a majority in the electoral college. Mr Trump's 306 electoral college votes ranked 46th in the 58 elections.

5. **11%.** The Senate was deliberately designed to balance the power of the large and small states. It was also designed, according to James Madison, to be a check on the House of Representatives and "protect the people against the transient impressions into which they themselves might be led". Originally, senators were chosen by state legislatures, rather than popularly elected.

6. **John Adams,** the second president. He and John Quincy Adams are the only two among the first dozen presidents not to own slaves and often hundreds of them, though Martin Van Buren only had one. After Zachary Taylor, slave-owning presidents fell out of favour until Andrew Johnson and Ulysses S. Grant, both former slave owners, got the top job.

7. **Alexis de Tocqueville.** To improve their career prospects after Louis Philippe took the French throne in 1830, de Tocqueville and Gustave de Beaumont visited America to study the penal system. The pair spent just nine months in America, visiting prisons across the country, before returning to France to submit their report. De Tocqueville then drew on his experience to write his masterpiece on American politics and culture.

8. **Montana.** The clash, called the Battle of the Greasy Grass by the Indians and also referred to as Custer's Last Stand, took place between the 7th Cavalry, led by General Custer, and a huge gathering of Sioux and Cheyenne warriors in 1876. Custer was unaware of the number of Indians under the command of Sitting Bull. His troops were outnumbered and quickly overwhelmed in an ignominious defeat that did not go unpunished.

9. **Morgan and Virgil**. The gunfight took place in Tombstone, Arizona, in 1881 and lasted about half a minute, during which time some 30 shots were fired. Doc Holliday was a dentist.

10. **Five**: Colorado, Idaho, Kansas, Nevada and North Dakota. Its presidential candidate was James B. Weaver. In 1896, the party backed the Democratic candidate, William Jennings Bryan, who campaigned against the gold standard. The party was an early example of anti-elitist populism.

11. **William Howard Taft,** who was president from 1909 to 1913 and Chief Justice from 1921 to 1930. He was also the heaviest president, hitting 152–154kg (335–340 pounds) at one stage.

12. **Three**. Teddy Roosevelt in 1906, Woodrow Wilson in 1919 and Jimmy Carter in 2002

13. **Just one day**. She was chosen as an honour by the state's governor after the incumbent died. A special election saw her immediately replaced. She was also the oldest freshman senator, taking her seat at age 87.

14. **Brent Bozell**, the brother-in-law of William F. Buckley Jr, who founded the *National Review*. Goldwater, the Republican nominee in 1964, was the inspiration for many modern Conservatives, and said in his convention

speech that "extremism in the defence of liberty is no vice". His slogan was "In your heart, you know he's right", but this was countered by Lyndon Johnson who quipped "In your guts, you know he's nuts". Johnson won in a landslide.

15. It lifted the **ban on interracial marriage**. Mildred and Richard Loving had been sentenced to a year in prison in Virginia for marrying each other.

16. **The Missouri** at 3,767km (2,341 miles).

17. **Hawaii** at 1,618mm (64 inches) a year and **Nevada** at 241mm.

18. **Wyoming** produced around 42% of the country's coal output in 2015, well ahead of West Virginia (11%), the state most usually associated with the fuel.

19. **Bureau of Land Management** (BLM), **Forest Service** (FS), **Fish and Wildlife Service** (FWS) and **National Park Service** (NPS). The federal government owns some 640 million acres of land in the United States and the four federal agencies manage 610 million acres as follows: BLM 248 million acres, FS 193 million acres; FWS 89 million acres; and NPS 80 million acres. Most of these lands are in the West and in Alaska.

20. **Alaska, Florida, Nevada, South Dakota, Texas, Washington, Wyoming.** All these states raise money for services through sales and property taxes and the like. Tennessee and New Hampshire come close. The states do not tax pay but do tax interest and dividends.

21. A worrying **30%** were unclear about where their chosen party stood. Only about a fifth of voters pay close attention to politics. For the rest, political issues are, as Robert Dahl, a noted political scientist, put it in 1961, "a sideshow in the great circus of life".

22. **26th.** The US is an outlier thanks to a system that inflates healthcare spending. Europeans, such as the Swiss and Italians, live more than four years longer.

23. **A one-piece swimming costume**. Reagan worked as a lifeguard at Lowell Park beach on the Rock River. He is credited with saving over 70 people from drowning, though there are suggestions that some young ladies may have faked their distress to attract the attention of the handsome young lifeguard.

24. **Sauerkraut**. The menus in some congressional office buildings changed the name of "French fries" to "freedom fries" in 2003 after France refused to support America in its stance over Iraq.

25. **St Louis, Missouri**. Eliot was a poet, dramatist and literary critic best known for his poem, *The Waste Land*. Chuck Berry was a poet of rock 'n' roll best known for "Johnny B. Goode" and "Roll Over Beethoven". Yogi Berra was a baseball catcher who appeared in 14 World Series for the New York Yankees and won 10 of them but is also known for his poetically daft utterances such as "When you come to a fork in the road, take it".

26. **The Dakota apartments** on the upper west side of Manhattan. The apartments were first built in the 1880s. John Lennon was murdered outside the block in 1980.

27. **Eighteen**. The boards date back to the 1920s and collected $58 million in taxes in 2011. America has a tradition of electing local officials.

28. **Seventeen**. Those states and parts of Alaska, Maryland, Minnesota and South Dakota control the wholesale sale of spirits and, in some cases, wine, through government agencies. Thirteen also control retail sales for home consumption through government-operated shops or appointed agents.

29. a) **North Carolina** b) **New Hampshire** c) **Wisconsin**.

30. **Nebraska**. It switched from a bicameral system in 1937.

31. **Lake Pontchartrain Causeway in Louisiana**, which is 38.4km (23.87 miles) long.

32. **One of the longest road tunnels in America**. The 1.6 mile (2.6km) tunnel was part of one of the most complex and pricey pieces of infrastructure engineering in America. The "Big Dig" included a bridge and several tunnels including the Ted Williams Tunnel, which opened in 1995.

33. a) **Idlewild in New York** b) **National in Arlington, Virginia** (it services Washington, DC) c) **Houston Intercontinental**.

34. **Louis Kahn**. He was born in Pärnu, Estonia, in 1901 and his family emigrated to America when he was a child. After studying architecture at the University of Pennsylvania and opening his own firm in 1935, it was many years before he was recognised as one of the greatest architects of the 20th century with buildings that also included the Yale University Art Gallery, Kimbell Art Museum and the capitol complex in Dhaka, Bangladesh. Kahn died in New York City in 1974.

35. **Eugene Cernan**. Cernan and Harrison Schmitt stepped out of the lunar module of *Apollo 17* and onto the moon in December 1972. In total only 12 people have done so. Cernan, commander of *Apollo 17*, also uttered the last words (so far) on the moon: "America's challenge of today has forged man's destiny of tomorrow. And, as we leave the Moon at Taurus-Littrow, we leave as we came and, God willing, as we shall return, with peace and hope for all mankind. Godspeed to the crew of *Apollo 17*."

36. **Hawaii**. The average life expectancy in America now stands at 78.9 years. But Hawaiians live for 81.3 years on average, just edging out Minnesotans who hang around for 81.1 years.

37. **2001**. A plurality (43%) approved in 1982 but approval fell during the AIDS crisis and only rebounded decisively around the turn of the millennium.

38. **Spruce Goose**. The plane, six-times larger than any that existed at the time, was built out of wood because of government restrictions on using

aluminium, which was needed for the war effort. It was conceived to ferry troops and war supplies across the Atlantic Ocean out of reach of German U-boats but arrived too late. Despite its name it was made mostly of birch.

39. a) **Michigan** b) **Ohio** c) **Alabama**.

40. a) **New Mexico** b) **Arizona** c) **Alaska**.

41. **2007**. There were fewer than 500 breeding pairs at one stage thanks to the impact of pesticides like DDT, loss of habitat and hunting.

42. The **Great Smoky Mountains** park on the border of North Carolina and Tennessee is the most visited site.

43. **Mount Saint-Elias**. Denali was formerly known as Mount McKinley. The 10 highest peaks are all in Alaska; the highest in the lower 48 states is Mount Whitney in California.

44. **Yupik**, with 19,000 speakers. Although there are an estimated 169 Native American languages, there are only around 370,000 speakers in total.

45. **Thirty-eight million**. The total Hispanic population was estimated at 55 million in 2014, or around 17% of the total for the United States.

46. **Near San Bernadino, California**. Mac and Dick McDonald originally sold barbecue but focused on hamburgers after 1948 and gradually made the outfit more specialised and efficient. Ray Kroc persuaded them to franchise the operation in 1954 and bought the brothers' interest for $2.7 million in 1961.

47. **R.E.M. and the B-52s.**

48. a) **Cleveland, Ohio** b) **Canton, Ohio** c) **Dayton, Ohio**. Ohio has 17 halls of fame in all, including ones for accounting and polka.

49. **(Bonnie) Parker** and **(Clyde) Barrow**. Played by Warren Beatty and Faye Dunaway in an Oscar-winning film, the pair graduated from petty theft to robbing banks and killing policemen in a spree lasing two years until they were shot and killed by cops in Louisiana in 1934. Their gang was probably responsible for 13 murders, including those of two policemen.

50. **Superbowl Sunday**, the final of the American football competition. In 2017, Americans consumed an estimated 1.3 billion chicken wings, 12.5 million pizzas and 86 million kgs (190 million lbs) of avocados on that day.

BENIGHTED KINGDOM: Britain

1. **Queen Elizabeth II,** whose coronation took place in 1952. Since the death of King Bhumibol Adulyadej of Thailand, she is also the world's longest-serving monarch.

2. **Twelve,** of whom Theresa May is the latest. Of them, nine have been Conservative, two Labour and one Liberal. Five went on to win a general election during their premiership.

3. **Stephen** (1135–1154) whose reign was marked by civil war and **John** (1199–1216) whose misrule led the barons to insist on the Magna Carta in 1215.

4. According the 2011 census **Muslims** are the second-largest religious group in England and Wales, making up 4.8% of the population, compared with 59.3% who identified as Christian. In a survey by Ipsos Mori, a pollster, Britons overestimated this by a factor of more than four.

5. **In the 1910s**; in 1918 Constance Markievicz became the first woman to be elected to Westminster but as an Irish republican she did not take her seat. The first woman to do so was Nancy Astor in 1919.

6. **Three**, in 1908, 1948 and 2012.

7. **Labour politician James Callaghan** between the years of 1964 and 1979. He is, however, best remembered for leading Britain through the "Winter of Discontent" in 1978–79.

8. **98%**, when investment income was included in 1974 (but only 750,000 paid it). It was cut to 40% by 1988 by Margaret Thatcher's government.

9. **Japanese**. The restaurant was a branch of Itsu on Piccadilly, near The Economist Tower.

10. **Queen Victoria**. She reigned from 1837 to 1901, longer than the average Briton's life expectancy at the time.

11. **King Edward VIII**, later the Duke of Windsor after his abdication. Along with his wife, the Duke visited Hitler in 1937; there was a plot by the Germans to install him as a puppet king in the event of a successful German invasion of Britain.

12. It was the first advanced country to **go to the IMF for a loan**.

13. **The Isle of Man, Jersey and Guernsey**. They have their own assemblies and are not part of the EU or the British Commonwealth.

14. **George H. W. Bush** of prime minister's questions, the now-weekly session in which the head of the government must answer questions from MPs.

15. **Lord Shelburne, the Duke of Wellington** (both born in Ireland before it became part of the union in 1801) and **Andrew Bonar Law**, who was born in Canada.

16. **They are both islands**, the Isle of Wight and Na h-Eileanan an Iar, part of the Highlands and Islands. The latter seat used to be known as the Western Isles.

17. **St Francis of Assisi** with the words "Where there is discord, may we bring harmony. Where there is error, may we bring truth. Where there is doubt, may we bring faith. And where there is despair, may we bring hope." In fact, he had been dead almost 700 years when the prayer was first printed, anonymously, by a French clerical magazine, *La Clochette*, in 1912. The real author was probably the magazine's editor, Father Esther Bouquerel.

18. a) **Oxford** (12 out of 23 who have held the office); b) **five** (David Lloyd George, Ramsay McDonald, Winston Churchill, James Callaghan and John Major).

19. **Nikita Khrushchev** banging his shoe on the table while MacMillan addressed the General Assembly of the United Nations on the subject of the UN's intervention in the former Belgian Congo.

20. **Africa**. He gave the speech to the Parliament of South Africa in Cape Town in 1960.

21. **In 1969** it was lowered to 18 for both men and women. Most men over the age of 21 had been able to vote since 1884 and women over the age of 21 since 1928.

22. They are **mountains over 3000 feet** in height, named after Sir Hugh Munro who first surveyed and catalogued them in the late nineteenth century. Over 6,000 people claim to have climbed (or walked up) the lot.

23. Historically it was the **chief whip** but today it houses the prime minister's press office and strategic communications unit. The upper floor forms part of the prime minister's apartment and the chief whip's office has been moved to 9 Downing Street.

24. **Chancellor of the exchequer**. Jacqui Smith, a Labour politician, was the first female home secretary in 2007; Margaret Beckett, also of the Labour Party, became the first female foreign secretary in 2006; and Margaret Thatcher was the first female prime minister in 1979.

25. **Welsh** with 562,000 speakers, only narrowly ahead of Polish, which at 546,000, is the most-spoken non-native language.

26. **Harold MacMillan**. A nephew of his wife, Lady Dorothy Cavendish, married Kathleen, a sister to Kennedy. She died before Kennedy became president.

27. He was an **osteopath** who treated a number of society figures including Lord Astor and Winston Churchill's son-in-law. A musical called *Stephen Ward* appeared in the West End in 2013; it was a rare flop for Andrew Lloyd Webber, the composer.

28. **Twenty-two**. Despite the book's title, not all of these were invasions as, in some cases, a British military presence occurred with the agreement of the local power and in others, action was purely naval.

29. **Spencer Perceval** on May 11, 1812. He was shot in the lobby of the House of Commons by John Bellingham, a merchant with an obsessive grievance against the government, who believed he had been unfairly imprisoned by the Russians and was owed compensation.

30. Only **5.9%**. Farmland covers more than half the country. If one looks at buildings alone, they cover just 1.4% of the land area, less than is revealed when the tide goes out.

31. a) **Andrew Bonar Law** b) **Anthony Eden** c) **Neville Chamberlain** d) **Benjamin Disraeli** e) **John Major**.

32. **Undersecretary of state for the colonies in 1905**. As such he was responsible for colonial affairs worldwide.

33. **Robber or brigand**. It is derived from the middle Irish word *tóraidhe*.

34. **Chequers in Buckinghamshire**, which was given to the nation via a Parliamentary Act of 1917. Up until then, prime minsters had tended to be drawn from the landed gentry, so had their own country estates.

35. **Medicine in 1865.** She was also a suffragist, the co-founder of the first hospital staffed by women, the first female dean of a British medical school and the first female doctor of medicine in France.

36. **The cod wars.** Iceland won.

37. They were the most **popular baby names** for boys and girls in 2016.

38. **Curry house.** He opened the Hindoostane Coffee House in Portman Square in London in 1810. Today the curry house is a British institution. Most are run by Bangladeshis; around two-fifths of working-age Bangladeshi men in Britain toil in restaurants. But changes in eating habits, stricter immigration rules and a better-educated British-Bangladeshi population mean the future of curry houses is uncertain.

39. In **1975** on the country's membership of the **European Community**. The vote was 67%–33% in favour of staying in.

40. **Stonehenge.** She didn't like it, so in 1918 he gave it to the nation.

41. a) Dessert. It is pastry filled with dried fruit and spices, often eaten with cream b) Starter. It is a Scottish soup made from haddock, potatoes and onions and c) Main course. It is sausages cooked in batter.

42. **Colgate toothpaste**.

43. **Denis Thatcher**. Thatcher never lived with his first wife, and they divorced after his demobilisation and return to England after the second world war in 1948.

 44. **New Orleans** with 62.7 inches. Even Orlando gets more rain than London, which averages only 23 inches. Admittedly, London gets a lot more cloudy days than the other two.

45. **The Big Bang**, Margaret Thatcher's sudden deregulation of the financial markets that largely created today's City (the common name for London's financial sector).

46. **Virginia Wade** in 1977. There were two female winners in the 1960s as well. The previous *male* winner was Fred Perry in 1936, but that wasn't the question.

47. **Friedrich Nietzsche**, a German philosopher of nihilism, known for his theory of the Übermensch.

48. a) **Tony Blair**, Labour, won a majority of **179** in 1997; b) **Tony Blair**, Labour, won a majority of **167** in 2001; and c) **Clement Atlee**, also Labour, won a majority of **146** in 1945.

49. The **unicorn**. Unconfirmed reports suggest that Scottish unicorns can be found living close to the Loch Ness monster.

50. The establishment in Palestine of **a national home for the Jewish people,** although it qualified this by saying that this should not prejudice non-Jewish communities.

OCCIDENTS OF HISTORY: Europe

1. **Zeus**. He had a habit of disguising himself to seduce women, also appearing as a satyr and a swan.

2. **King Minos of Crete**, who sacrificed Athenians to a half-man, half-bull called the Minotaur in the Labyrinth.

3. **Jupiter**. It was one of the four moons to be discovered by Galileo. At the time of writing, astronomers have discovered 69 moons of Jupiter in all.

4. The **president of the European Central Bank**. As of early 2018, this was Mario Draghi.

5. **Latin**, **Greek** and **Cyrillic**, added in 2013 after Bulgaria joined the EU.

6. a) **Finland** b) **Italy** c) **France**.

7. **Estonia** and **Iceland**. The figures are based on Gini coefficients, which measure the distribution of income; a coefficient of 1 means that all the income is owned by one person. As the coefficient falls towards zero, income is more evenly distributed. Estonia was at 0.36, Iceland at 0.24.

8. **Tiny Monaco** was the most densely occupied country in the world, never mind Europe, in 2015, with over 25,000 people per square km (64,750 per square mile), according to the UN. Malta was the most densely occupied EU nation, at 1,308 people per square km; lovers of wide-open spaces should head for Iceland, the least densely populated European nation, at 3.3 people per square km, or Finland, the least crowded EU nation at 18.1.

9. **24**. Bulgarian, Croatian, Czech, Danish, Dutch, English, Estonian, Finnish, French, German, Greek, Hungarian, Irish, Italian, Latvian, Lithuanian, Maltese, Polish, Portuguese, Romanian, Slovak, Slovene, Spanish and Swedish. Another 60 regional languages, such as Catalan and Frisian, are also spoken.

10. **The latest estimate, as of 2010, was 6%**, on the way up to 8% by 2030. This puts the talk in some parts of the press of "Eurabia" into context. Cyprus, once part of the Ottoman Empire, had the highest proportion of Muslims in the EU at 25%. Surveys show that the public wildly overestimates the proportion; in France and Belgium, people thought that around 30% of citizens were Muslim, four to five times the actual figure.

11. **Nine**: Belgium, Denmark, Liechtenstein, Luxembourg, Monaco, the Netherlands, Norway, Spain and Sweden. The longest serving (as of May 2017) was Queen Margrethe II of Denmark, on the throne since 1972.

12. a) **Charles** (or **Karl**) I (abdicated 1918) b) **Umberto II** (deposed 1946) c) **Manuel II** (deposed 1910) d) **Constantine II** (deposed 1973).

13. **Louis Napoleon Bonaparte**, nephew of the first Napoleon. He was elected President of the Republic in 1848 and became Emperor Napoleon III via a coup in 1851. (The first emperor had declared his son Napoleon II when he abdicated in 1814.) The second empire ended when France was defeated in the Franco-Prussian war.

14. The **Eurovision Song Contest**, held every year since 1956. Abba and Celine Dion have been among the winners. Voting is by viewers and national juries, who can be highly political. Portugal won the contest in 2017.

15. **Finland** with 73%.

16. a) **Albania**, b) **Cyprus** and c) **Macedonia**.

17. **Francis II** who dissolved the empire in 1806, after defeat by Napoleon. The empire was a patchwork of cities, bishoprics and dynastic holdings with much of its territory in modern Germany; Voltaire quipped it was "neither holy, nor Roman nor an empire". After its dissolution, the power of the ruling Habsburg family shifted to the Austro-Hungarian empire, which survived until 1918.

18. **Finland** granted female suffrage in 1906, although in global terms it lagged behind both New Zealand and Australia. A rash of countries granted women the vote after the first world war but Switzerland held out until 1971 and **Portuguese** women had to wait for the fall of the right-wing Estado Novo regime; they received full suffrage in 1976.

19. **Finland** at 58%; the EU average was 46.6%.

20. **Ireland** at 28%.

21. The **European Commission**, the **European Parliament**, the **European Council** and (confusingly) the **Presidency of the Council of the European Union**. This last post is taken by member governments for six months, on a rotating basis. The President of the European Council is chosen by member states for 2.5 years at a stretch (at the time of writing, it was Donald Tusk of Poland). The Commission is the EU's civil service.

22. a) The **war of the Spanish Succession** b) the **Napoleonic wars** c) the **Franco-Prussian war**.

⚠ 23. Charles **the Bald** (843–77 CE), **the Fat** (885–88), **the Simple** (898–922) and **the Wise** (1364–80).

24. a) **The Netherlands**. The short-lived Batavian Republic was established under French revolutionary rule; it lasted from 1795 to 1806 until Napoleon established the Kingdom of Holland with his brother Louis as monarch. b) **Britain**. This was the Kingdom of Strathclyde which ruled over western Scotland and northern England in early medieval times. c) **Switzerland**. Another of Napoleon's creations, this lasted only from 1798 to 1803 until the cantonal structure was restored.

25. a) **Belgium**—it's a Flemish nationalist group b) **Spain**—a left-wing party c) **Czech Republic**—a conservative pro-EU group d) **The Netherlands**—a socially liberal party.

26. **Seven**: Serbia, Croatia, Bosnia and Herzegovina, Slovenia, Montenegro, Macedonia and Kosovo.

27. **Joining the EU.**

28. a) **North Rhine-Westphalia** b) **Bremen.**

29. a) **Bavaria** b) **Bremen.**

30. 26. The number has grown over the years; the origins of the structure can be traced as far back as the federal charter of 1291.

31. a) **French, German, Italian** and **Romansh** b) **Latin**.

32. **Liechtenstein**.

33. a) **Bulgaria** b) **Czechoslovakia** c) **Hungary**.

34. a) He was a **chemist** who invented a form of plastic known as Bakelite. b) He was a **cyclist** who won the Tour de France five times. c) When she changed her name to Audrey Hepburn, she became a **Hollywood actress**.

35. a) **Potsdam**. It was the summer palace of Frederick the Great, King of Prussia. b) **Munich**. It was built in the 17th century for the electors of Bavaria. c) **Apeldoorn** in the Netherlands. It was built in the late 17th century for William of Orange and Mary II of Britain.

36. **Vienna in 1913**. Tito and Trotsky were in the city at the same time.

37. a), b) and c) are **Stalin**; d) is from **Hitler**.

38. 26. The largest is Cork at 7,457km^2 (2,879 miles^2); the smallest is Louth at 820km^2.

39. a) **Loire** b) **Burgundy** c) **Bordeaux**.

40. **France, Belgium, Italy** and **Switzerland**.

41. a) **Norway** and **Sweden**. Sweden had been awarded Norway as a reward for joining the Allied fight against Napoleon; the two countries had a common monarch and foreign policy but had separate legislatures and currencies. b) **Belgium** and **the Netherlands**. Another result of the Napoleonic settlement, the Dutch crown reunited the two areas once ruled by the Habsburg monarchy. But Belgium revolted in favour of independence in 1830. The treaty recognising Belgium's borders, signed in 1839, was the "scrap of paper" that pushed Britain into the first world war. c) **Germany** and **Austria**. The two countries were united by the *anschluss* of 1938, much to the delight of Adolf Hitler, who was born in Austria. They were separated again after the war.

42. **Avignon in France**. The powerful French monarchy installed seven successive French popes in the 14th century and, after Gregory XI moved back to Rome, appointed rival or antipopes. The schism only ended in 1417.

43. a) **Rotterdam** b) **Budapest** c) **Lisbon**.

44. a) **Alexander II** in 1861. This was not as magnanimous as it sounded; the serfs had to buy the land they worked, resulting in a lot of debt. b) **Alexander I**, who also allied with Napoleon for a while. In 1815 he formed the Holy Alliance with Austria and Prussia to preserve the rights of absolute monarchs. c) **Nicholas I**. He died in the course of the war—which did not end well for Russia. His successor, Alexander II, had to give up a Black Sea fleet to end the conflict.

45. The European court of Human Rights, based in Strasbourg, France. The court was set up in 1959 to protect the right of citizens in countries that adopted the European Convention on Human Rights.

 46. a) East Germany b) Hungary and c) Czechoslovakia.

47. **France** (in first place), **Spain** (in third) and **Italy** (fifth).

48. a) **Spain** at 83.3 b) **Bulgaria** and **Latvia** at 74.5. Latvian males have a life expectancy of just 69.1 years.

49. a) **Nero**, who committed suicide in 68 CE, having been declared a public enemy by the senate. b) **Trajan**, who ruled from 98–117 CE. He conquered Armenia, Dacia and Mesopotamia. c) **Valerian** was captured after the battle of Edessa in 260 CE. Lactantius told the footstool story. Some sources claim Valerian was flayed alive; others that he was forced to swallow molten gold.

50. **Poland**, which was divided between Austria, Prussia and Russia. It was divided again between Germany and the Soviet Union in 1939.

LATIN QUARTER: The Americas

1. **Tenochtitlan**. It was captured by Hernán Cortés in 1521 with the help of local allies and after the Aztec defenders had been devastated by a smallpox epidemic.

2. **Cacao beans**. In 1555, the Spanish adopted an exchange rate of 140 beans to the *real*. The beans were still being used as small change in the 1850s.

3. It was a court for **a violent sport**, roughly resembling basketball, in which the aim was to get a ball though a stone hoop. At Chichén Itzá in Mexico, reliefs appear to show the winners holding aloft the severed head of a member of the losing team. In modern basketball, this would be regarded as a personal foul.

4. The dividing line between **Spanish and Portuguese possessions in the New World**. The line was drawn 1,360 miles (2,189km) west of the Cape Verde islands off the coast of Africa. As it happened, the coast of Brazil was east of the line, bringing it under Portuguese control. The rest of the Americas, on this basis, belonged to Spain, although other European powers did not accept the deal.

5. **Potosí**, where silver was mined. The town, founded in 1545, had 200,000 inhabitants at one stage.

6. **Six**. Bolívar, known as El Libertador or The Liberator, was born in modern-day Venezuela (which named its currency after him). He started his campaign for independence in 1808, when Spain was weakened by the Napoleonic wars. He was a strong believer in a broader Latin American state, acting as president of Gran Colombia (which covered Venezuela, Colombia, Panama and Ecuador) from 1819 to 1830. In addition to those four, Peru and Bolivia are considered Bolivarian countries; he was president of both.

7. **Chile**. He was the son of Ambrose (later Ambrosio) O'Higgins, an Irishman who emigrated to Latin America, and became royal governor of Chile and viceroy of Peru. Bernardo rebelled against Spanish rule and became supreme director of Chile in 1817, before being deposed in a coup in 1823.

8. **Guano**, or bird droppings, which were prized in Europe as a fertiliser. Eventually the deposits ran out and artificial fertilisers were developed.

9. **Nine**, starting with Isabel Perón in Argentina in 1974. She was the third wife of Juan Perón, a general who was elected three times as president. His second wife, Eva, was immortalised in the musical, *Evita*. Other female presidents have been Lidia Gueiler Tejada (Bolivia), Violeta Chamorro

(Nicaragua), Rosalia Arteaga (Ecuador), Mireya Moscoso (Panama), Michelle Bachelet (Chile), Cristina Fernandez de Kirchner (Argentina), Laura Chinchilla (Costa Rica) and Dilma Rousseff (Brazil).

10. **Napoleon III of France**. Maximilian was the younger brother of Francis Joseph, the long-serving emperor of Austria-Hungary. He was eventually captured and executed by Mexican forces who restored Benito Juárez as president. Napoleon III didn't last that much longer, succumbing to defeat by the Germans in 1870.

11. **71 years**, from 1929 to 2000. The party only took its current name in 1946, having previously been known as the National Revolutionary Party and the Party of the Mexican Revolution. The party and state were closely linked, especially after the nationalisation of the oil industry before the second world war. By 2000, the party was associated with corruption and lost power. But it returned to power in 2012 under President Enrique Peña Nieto.

12. **Argentina**, **Brazil** and **Uruguay**. The war was initiated by the dictatorial Francisco Solano López, a Paraguayan president who banned people from turning their backs on him or sitting while he stood. The Paraguayans were hopelessly mismatched and it is estimated that 60% of the population, or 90% of its men, died directly from the conflict, or from diseases and starvation caused by it.

13. **Chile**. The film received four Oscar nominations and jointly won the Palme d'Or at the Cannes festival. It is set in the aftermath of the military coup of 1973.

14. **Brazil in 1888**. Brazil imported more slaves (around 4 million) than any other country in the Atlantic slave-trade era, largely to work on sugar plantations.

⚠ 15. **Friedrich Nietzsche's sister**, Elizabeth, and her husband Bernhard Förster. The colony, called Nueva Germania, was founded in 1887. Förster committed suicide in 1889, and his wife went back to Germany. German is still spoken by some families in the area.

16. **São Paulo, Brazil**. There are an estimated 1.5 million people of Japanese descent in Brazil. Many of them came over in the first half of the 20th century to work on coffee plantations. There are two Japanese-language newspapers in São Paulo.

17. **Bolivia, Brazil, Colombia, Ecuador, French Guiana, Guyana, Peru, Suriname, Venezuela**.

18. **20%**. The rainforest is also home to 40,000 plant species, 1,300 bird species and 2.5 million types of insects. At 5.5 million km² (2.12 million miles²), it is almost twice the size of India.

19. **The Parana**, which runs 4,880km (3,032 miles) through Brazil, Paraguay and Argentina.

20. **Lake Titicaca**, on the border of Bolivia and Peru. The lake has an area of 8,372km^2 (3,232 miles^2) and is 3,812 metres (12,506 feet) above sea level. Bolivia's second-largest lake, Lake Poopó, has dried up and there are fears for the long-term health of Titicaca, if global warming continues.

21. **The Sargasso Sea**. All other seas are partly bounded by land, while the Sargasso Sea is delineated only by ocean currents. It lies within the Northern Atlantic subtropical gyre, the Gulf Stream, the North Atlantic current, the Canary Current and the North Atlantic equatorial current. It is named after sargassum, abundant free-floating seaweed that is also a spawning ground for white marlin, porbeagle shark and dolphinfish. *Wide Sargasso Sea*, a novel by the Dominica-born Jean Rhys, is a prequel to *Jane Eyre*.

22. **Peru**. The Nazca Lines, a UN heritage site, form pictures of animals, trees and geometric shapes. They can be seen from surrounding hills and are believed to have religious significance; the Nazca civilisation lasted from around 500 BCE to 500 CE. Wilder speculation about the purpose of the lines is out there, with some arguing they are airfields for space aliens.

23. La Paz in Bolivia at 3,650 metres (11,975 feet) above sea level. It was founded by the Spanish in 1548. Its official name is Nuestra Señora de La Paz (Our Lady of Peace).

24. Chihuahua at 247,000km^2 (95,000 miles^2). Excluding Mexico City, Tlaxcala is the smallest at 4,000km^2.

25. 26, plus the federal district of Brasilia. The origins of the states date back to Portuguese colonisation, and the hereditary captaincies granted to noblemen and merchants. The largest is Amazonas at 1.57 million km^2 (606,000 miles^2); São Paulo is the most heavily populated.

26. A trillion reais. As Brazil battled with inflation, it changed the name and denomination of its currency. Between 1980 and 1997, the *cruzeiro* became the *cruzado* and eventually the *real*, the name of the original post-colonial currency. In 1990 alone, inflation exceeded 30,000%.

27. Import substitution industrialisation. The theory was that developing countries had been trapped into producing raw materials for the developed world. The volatility of commodity prices placed them in a weak position. The aim was to industrialise and that had to be done via tariffs to exclude foreign products.

28. **To manage the economy**. It didn't work that well; Chile descended into hyperinflation, suffered a decline in GDP in 1972 and 1973 and workers saw their real wages squeezed. Allende was ousted in a coup in 1973.

29. **Alfredo Stroessner**, a general who ruled Paraguay from 1954 to 1989. He was ousted in a coup by his second-in-command and went into exile into Brazil, dying in 2006 at the age of 93.

30. **Argentina**. As many as 30,000 Argentinians were "disappeared" during the era, as a military junta hunted down left-wing dissidents.

31. **The United Fruit Company**. The firm was enormously powerful in Central America and its hold over governments led to some being dubbed "banana republics". As the largest land owner in Guatemala, the company was threatened by a programme of land reform. The government offered to compensate UFC for the land based on the value the group had declared for tax purposes.

32. The Fuerzas Armadas Revolucionarias de Colombia were founded in 1964 by **Manuel Marulanda Vélez** as the armed wing of the Communist movement. The FARC funded itself by kidnapping, extortion and drug running. It disarmed in June 2017.

33. **Abimael Guzmán**, a university professor, founded the group in the 1960s. It took its name from an adage of the founder of the Peruvian Communist Party—"Marxism-Leninism will open the shining path to revolution". In Spanish, shining path is *sendero luminoso*. Although Guzmán was captured in 1992, the Shining Path still carries out occasional attacks.

34. **Haiti** is the least equal as measured by the Gini coefficient (a ranking of 1 would mean a single person earned all the income; Haiti is at 0.61). Only South Africa and Namibia are less equal. The most egalitarian country in the region, unsurprisingly, is **Canada** with a coefficient of 0.34.

35. a) **Peru** b) **Guatemala** c) **Jamaica**.

36. **Ten** (Alberta, British Columbia, Manitoba, New Brunswick, Newfoundland and Labrador, Nova Scotia, Ontario, Prince Edward Island, Quebec and Saskatchewan). The largest is **Quebec** and the smallest **Prince Edward Island**.

37. **Newfoundland in 1949**. The region did not join the original confederation but was independent until it hit a debt crisis in the 1930s; after 1934, it was ruled from Britain. Newfoundlanders voted to join Canada in a referendum in July 1948, but only by 52% to 48%.

38. a) **Saskatchewan** b) **Prince Edward Island** c) **Ontario**.

39. **Nine**, five by Brazil (1958, 1962, 1970, 1994 and 2002), two by Argentina (1978 and 1986) and two by Uruguay (1930 and 1950). The other 11 world cups (up to 2014) have all been won by European teams.

40. a) **1916** and b) **Uruguay** with 15 wins. Until 1975, the tournament was known as the Campeonato Sudamericano de Fútbol (South American Football Championship).

41. a) and b) are both **São Paulo**, c) is **Rio de Janeiro**. Palmeiras has been the most successful club, winning the national league nine times.

42. **Jamaica**. The first song to use the term was "Do the Reggay" by Toots and the Maytals in 1968. Its most famous musician was Bob Marley (1945–1981).

43. **Grenada**, the **Bahamas** and **Jamaica** in that order. The region has a great record in sprinting, with all its medals earned in distances of 400 metres or less. The star, of course, was Usain Bolt of Jamaica, who won the 100 metres and 200 metres for three games in succession.

44. **Frida Kahlo**, best known for her self-portraits which formed 55 of her 143 paintings. Her relationship with Rivera was tempestuous; in *Self-Portrait with Chopped Hair*, she illustrates the times she cut off her hair when her husband was unfaithful.

45. It was commissioned for the **Rockefeller Center** in New York. But the Marxist Rivera included a picture of Lenin and a Soviet May Day parade. Nelson Rockefeller (later the vice-president) had the work destroyed in 1934.

46. **Jorge Luis Borges.** Borges, born in Buenos Aires in 1899, began publishing poems and essays in surrealist literary journals in the 1920s and his best-known works, *Fictions* and *The Aleph* in the 1940s. He did not come to worldwide attention until 1961 when he shared the prestigious literary award, the Prix Formentor, with Samuel Beckett.

 47. a) **Panama** b) **Mexico** c) **Colombia**.

48. a) **Cuba** b) **Brazil** (although the roots of the dance are probably African) c) **Argentina**. Europeans and Americans adapted the dance for ballroom competitions but retain Argentine tango as a separate discipline.

49. **Colombia, Honduras, Mexico** and **Guatemala**. Brazil produces more than all four put together.

50. **Caipirinha**. Though its origins are unclear, some say that it first appeared as a medicine to lessen the effects of the Spanish flu that swept the planet at the end of the first world war. The original recipe included cachaça, lemon, honey and garlic. Cachaça, made from the fermented juice of sugar cane, is similar to rum.

TO UR IS HUMAN: Middle East and Africa

1. Its 1.2 billion inhabitants represent about **one-sixth** of the world's population. While population growth has slowed in much of the world, Africa is projected to see a slight acceleration in its growth in the immediate future.

2. **Saudi Arabia** which in 2016 produced 12.3 billion barrels a day.

3. a) **Ghana** b) **Botswana** c) **Swaziland** d) **Sao Tome and Principe** e) **Eritrea**.

4. **About 2,000**. They include English, French, Arabic, Xhosa, Swahili, Yoruba, Igbo, Zulu and Shona.

 5. **Flowers**. Kenya is the world's third-largest producer of cut flowers and the crop is its second-largest export, after tea.

6. The **British** and **French** governments respectively appointed them in 1916 to apportion the lands of what had been the **Ottoman Empire**, and which now form much of the modern Middle East.

7. Bahrain, Iran and **Iraq**. They also form the plurality (but not the majority) in Lebanon. Beyond the Middle East, Azerbaijan is also a Shia-majority country.

8. a) **the base or foundation** b) **the awakening** c) **youth**.

9. Syria, Iran, Iraq and **Turkey**. The Kurds run the semi-autonomous region of northern Iraq but still dream of an independent Kurdistan.

10. It is the **home of Jacob Zuma,** South Africa's fourth president since independence, and the location of his private estate on which he has lavished $24 million, much of it public money, on among other things an amphitheatre, a swimming pool and a cattle enclosure.

11. Cairo, in Arabic "um al-dunya".

12. 1962.

13. In the Tunisian town of **Sidi Bouzid** where a young man, Muhammad Bouazizi, set himself on fire, sparking the protests and the uprising that brought down the regime of Zine el-Abidine Ben Ali.

14. The Iranian government of **Mohammad Mossadegh**, in a coup orchestrated by America and Britain. They were worried, among other things, about the enthusiasm of the prime minister, who was democratically elected, when it came to the nationalisation of Iran's oil.

15. **Maronite Christian, Sunni Muslim** and **Shia Muslim**. Lebanon's democracy rests on a division of power between its 17 officially recognised religious "sects".

16. **Oslo** in 1993. The Oslo Accords laid out a peace process between the two sides and marked the first time that they officially recognised each other.

17. **South Sudan**, which gained independence from Sudan in 2011 and whose creation marked the end of Africa's longest-running civil war.

18. **Naguib Mahfouz**, a Egyptian writer, known for his great novels such as the Cairo Trilogy.

19. It was the **number assigned to Nelson Mandela** during his 27 years of imprisonment on Robben Island.

20. **It rebased its GDP**, leading to an 89% increase overnight. Sceptics might worry about such a leap, but in fact it was the old figures that were dodgy.

21. **The assassination of Anwar Sadat**. Mr Mubarak ruled for three decades before he was overthrown in the Egyptian revolution of 2011.

22. **Egypt** (known then as the United Arab Republic), **Jordan** and **Syria**.

23. **The 1920s in Egypt**. It was established by Hassan al-Banna, a school teacher, and has since spread throughout the Middle East.

24. They are the sites of Iran's two **uranium enrichment facilities**.

25. **Algeria**.

26. **Al Azhar in Cairo**, Egypt. Islam has no equivalent of the Pope or the Vatican but Al Azhar mosque and university form the Islamic world's most prestigious seat of learning.

27. **d) 1932**. The founder of the modern state was Abdul Aziz bin Saud and the crown has been passed to his descendants since then.

28. **Three**. Today at least 25 qualify and many more hold imperfect but worthwhile elections.

29. **The International Criminal Court**. Following a presidential election, the Gambia rescinded its withdrawal; the High Court of South Africa has ruled the country's withdrawal unlawful, but it is still committed to leaving the court and others may follow.

30. 231,000,000% (231 million percent). The country had to issue notes as large as the 100 trillion Zimbabwe-dollar bill—worth around 40 cents at the time of their demise.

31. **President of Cameroon since 1982.** He is the world's longest-serving non-royal national leader (if you count an early stint as prime minister).

32. **They are all within one country**; it is an enclave entirely surrounded by South Africa.

 33. **An African passport.** The first two holders were Paul Kagame, the president of Rwanda, and Idriss Déby, the president of Chad. It hopes to roll it out more widely to facilitate travel throughout the continent.

34. d) **an international area under UN control.** The status of Jerusalem remains one of the main points of conflict between the Israelis and Palestinians.

35. **Yom Kippur**, the feast of atonement. That year it also fell during the Muslim month of Ramadan.

36. **Saudi Arabia** and the **United Arab Emirates.** The non-Arab nation was **Pakistan.**

37. Binyamin Netanyahu. The two became friends but, unfortunately for Mr Netanyahu, Mr Romney failed to win the American presidency.

38. Just over a quarter (28%). They make up a significant proportion of those unemployed in the region, thought to be one of the factors that contributed to the uprisings of the Arab Spring.

39. Qatar. The satellite television channel, which launched in 2006, revolutionised Arab news coverage but has since been criticised by everyone from Syria to Libya to America. In mid-2017 other Arab nations tried to get Qatar to close the channel down.

40. a) **Belgium** b) **Belgium** c) **Portugal** d) **Britain**.

41. Mark Thatcher, son of Margaret Thatcher, was involved in the "Wonga Coup" in Equatorial Guinea to overthrow President Teodoro Obiang Nguema. The plot failed and President Obiang remains in charge.

42. Chad.

43. Eight years. At least half a million people were killed and Saddam used chemical weapons against the Iranians and his own people, the Kurds of Halabja.

44. David Ben-Gurion, the first prime minister of the modern state of Israel.

45. **The Empty Quarter**. It straddles Saudi Arabia, Oman, the United Arab Emirates and Yemen and is the world's largest sand desert.

46. **Haile Selassie**. He gave Ethiopia its first written constitution, which restricted the powers of parliament. He was overthrown in a military coup in 1974 and died in prison in 1975. He is revered as a messiah by Rastafarians.

47. b) **His nephew**, who shot him at point blank range during a royal audience. He was later declared officially insane.

48. **It does not have one**. Instead it has several "Basic Laws".

49. **Michel Foucault**, who demonstrated great enthusiasm for Khomeini's Islamic revolution upon the latter's return to Iran.

50. **20.4%**. Despite its size, with 1.2 billion people, the continent has fewer citizens than China.

EAST SIDERS: Asia

1. **Alma-Ata in Kazakhstan**. In 1854 the Russians built Verniy, a fort in the foothills of the Tien Shan mountains. In 1921 a vote changed the name of the city to Alma-Ata, which means "father of apples" and in 1929 the city became the capital of Kazakhstan, home to the forebears of many modern apple varieties. The apples in supermarkets are probably descended from those that still grow wild in the country.

2. **Singapore**. The Malay word *Singapura* is borrowed from Sanskrit. The kingdoms of south-east Asia and Indonesia were influenced by the spread of Indian civilisation, and the region's languages have also borrowed heavily from Sanskrit. The Sanskrit word also lives on in *Singh*, which makes up part of the name of every male Sikh.

3. **Bangkok**. Translated as "village of wild plums", Bangkok was the original site of the capital city located across the Chao Phraya river from the present-day capital. In 1782, King Rama I founded his new capital, Krung Thep ("The City of Angels"), in a position that could be better defended. The full name of the city is in fact Krung Thep Mahanakhon Amon Rattanakosin Mahinthara Ayuthaya Mahadilok Phop Noppharat

Ratchathani Burirom Udomratchaniwet Mahasathan Amon Piman Awatan Sathit Sakkathattiya Witsanukam Prasit.

4. **Kuala Lumpur**. Chinese prospectors in search of tin set up camp in 1857, at the spot where Kuala Lumpur now stands. Within a month most of them had died of malaria and other tropical diseases. But the tin they discovered brought in more miners and Kuala Lumpur quickly became a boomtown.

5. **Myanmar**. In 2005 the country's then military rulers moved the capital from Yangon to a new purpose-built site, constructed in secret in the middle of nowhere. In 1970 the military junta had also sowed confusion by suddenly switching the country from driving on the left to driving on the right, although most cars were right-hand drive.

6. **Bhutan**. The remote mountain kingdom on the edge of the Himalayas did away with using economic growth as a yardstick for development and enshrined GNH as the measure of development in the constitution of 2008.

7. **East Pakistan**. In 1971 a war between India and Pakistan spilled over into a battle for independence in East Pakistan, which led to the secession of the country and the creation of the state of Bangladesh.

8. **Strait of Malacca**. By linking the Indian Ocean and the South China Sea, the Strait of Malacca is the shortest sea route between India and China. It

is therefore one of the busiest shipping channels in the world. Singapore sits at the strait's southern end.

 9. Russia. The Russo-Japanese war was fought to establish dominance over Korea and Manchuria in China. The Russian government sent its Baltic fleet all the way to the other side of the planet to link up with its Pacific squadron. The Baltic fleet took over six months to reach its destination where it was soundly beaten by the Japanese.

10. Nepal. It is the only national flag which is not a quadrilateral. The design is based on pennants of rival branches of the Rana dynasty, which once ruled the country. The two designs were combined and adopted as the official flag in 1962, along with a constitutional government. The moon in the upper triangle represents the royal house. The sun in the lower part symbolises another branch of the Rana family.

11. Yellow River and the **Mekong.** The Yangtze, which stretches over 3,900 miles (6,276km) from Shanghai through the heart of China, is the world's third-longest river. The Yellow river, or Huang He, is known as the "mother river" of China and flows 3,400 miles from Qinghai province in western China to the Bohai Sea. The course of the Mekong takes it 3,050 miles from the Tibetan plateau in China through Myanmar, Laos, Thailand, Cambodia and Vietnam.

12. **K2** and **Kangchenjunga**. K2, also known as Mount Godwin-Austen or Chhogori, is located in the Karakoram range on the China–Pakistan border and is 28,250 feet (8,611 metres) in height. Kangchenjunga, at 28,200 feet, lies on the border between Nepal and the Indian state of Sikkim.

13. Attain the rank of **Sumo grand champion** or Yokozuna. Japan has not bred a grand champion since 1998. All those since have come from Mongolia or American Samoa.

14. **It can be deadly**. Fugu, or puffer fish, is a delicacy, served in wafer-thin slices at the best sushi restaurants. But the intestines, ovaries and liver contain a poison called tetrodotoxin and chefs must undergo three years of training to get a licence to prepare the fish for diners.

15. **Nara** and **Kyoto**. Japan's capital was the hometown of the emperor and when he died the ancients believed that the place of death was stricken with eternal bad luck and the capital was moved from place to place. Nara became Japan's permanent capital in 710. In 794 Emperor Kammu moved the seat of government to Kyoto. It remained the capital until the Imperial Restoration in 1868.

16. **Tokyo** was the venue for the summer Olympics in **1964**. But the last games held in the country were in **1998**, when the winter Olympics took place in **Nagano**. The winter games were also held in Sapporo in 1972.

17. **Flower arranging**. Ikebana derives from the Buddhist ritual of offering flowers to the spirits of the dead. The Japanese have raised it to the status of an art form.

18. **Busan**. The population of Seoul is over 10 million. Busan, located on the south-east coast at the mouth of South Korea's longest waterway, the Nakdong river, is home to 3.6 million people.

 19. **Pol Pot**. Pol Pot's communist Khmer Rouge led Cambodia from 1975 to 1979. Around 1.5 million (or perhaps even more) died of starvation and disease or were executed by a brutal regime trying to create a classless peasant society. A Vietnamese army force deposed the Khmer Rouge in 1979 and, after several years in hiding, Pol Pot died in 1998 under house arrest.

20. **Four**. Yap, Chuuk, Pohnpei and Kosrae. Together they make up around 600 islands in the Pacific.

21. **Hindi, Bengali, Telugu, Marathi, Tamil**. Over 422 million Indians speak Hindi. There are some 83 million Bengali speakers. Telugu, the language of Andhra Pradesh and Telangana, is spoken by 74 million. Marathi, predominantly spoken in Maharashtra, claims 72 million speakers. And Tamil is mainly spoken in Tamil Nadu as well as Sri Lanka. But taking into account second and third languages, English is the number two language in India.

22. Goa. Vasco da Gama first arrived in Goa in 1498 and it came under the rule of the Portuguese in 1510, who wanted to establish a trading post in India. The Portuguese stayed for nearly five centuries and refused to budge even after the rest of India gained independence in 1947. In December 1961 the Indian army crossed into Goa, and Portugal finally lost its grip on the territory.

23. Turkmenistan. Niyazov styled himself the Turkmenbashi, or "father of Turkmen", and like most dictators, looted his country's wealth. He spent much of it building up a bizarre personality cult. Ashgabat, the capital, was awash with giant portraits and gold statues of the man including one that constantly revolved through 360 degrees, so that it always faced the sun.

24. Uzbekistan. The country is surrounded by Afghanistan, Kazakhstan, Kyrgyzstan, Tajikistan and Turkmenistan, none of which have coastlines on open sea, so is also –stan locked. There are only two double landlocked countries in the world. The other is Liechtenstein, which is surrounded by Austria and Switzerland.

25. The first Indochina war of 1946–54. After the second world war France hoped to hang on to Vietnam, its former colonial possession. Ho Chi Minh, leader of the communists, declared independence in 1945. After a long guerrilla war his Viet Minh forces attacked 13,000 entrenched French troops at Dien Bien Phu, and after a siege lasting 57 days the French were defeated, ending their colonial rule in Indochina. America stepped into the gap and another long war began.

26. **Hue**. The city, located in central Vietnam, became the capital when Gia Long, the first of the Nguyen dynasty emperors, chose the location for his imperial city. The citadel, enclosed by thick walls and surrounded by a moat, and the tombs of Nguyen kings in the nearby area, have been classified by UNESCO as a world heritage site. The capital was moved in 1945 after Bao Dai, last of the Nguyen emperors, abdicated and a communist government was established in Hanoi.

27. **The kip**. The Free Lao kip was briefly introduced in 1945 before the French colonial powers took control and replaced it with the piaster. The "royal" kip was reintroduced in 1952 and lasted until 1976 when the Pathet Lao kip marked the communist movement's takeover of the country. After rapid inflation, this was replaced by the new kip in 1979 at a ratio of 100:1. The 500 kip note is the smallest denomination in circulation and the country uses no coins.

28. **Siem Reap**. The vast expanse of Angkor in northern Cambodia is probably the most important archaeological site in south-east Asia. It was once the centre of the Khmer Kingdom and is littered with temples such as Angkor

Wat, water courses and other structures. Siem Reap today is a major tourist destination, full of hotels and restaurants that cater to visitors to the ancient site.

29. **Squash**. Mr Khan first won the world title in 1987 and dominated the sport thereafter. He not only won eight world titles, the last in 1996 (and lost in the final once to his Pakistani rival Jahangir Khan in 1988), but also won the prestigious British Open six times between 1992 and 1997. But some say that Jahangir was the better player. He won the world title six times, the British Open a record ten times and went on a 555-match unbeaten run that lasted five years.

30. **Lollywood**. Bollywood is so called because the main centre of Indian film making is Mumbai, the name by which Bombay is now known. The Pakistan's film industry has a strong presence in Lahore, earning it the nickname Lollywood, though Karachi now rivals Lahore for prominence.

31. The **Gobi desert** covers 1.3 million km^2 (502,000 miles^2) of both southern Mongolia and parts of north and north-west China and is still expanding. Its dry climate is attributable to its position in the lee of the Himalayas, which blocks rain-laden clouds from reaching most of the Gobi. The desert is a valuable source of dinosaur fossils including the first ever discovery of dinosaur eggs. Gobi means "large and dry" in the Mongolian language.

32. **King Philip II of Spain**. Philip was king of Spain from 1556 to 1598. Yet in 1543 Ruy López de Villalobos, an explorer, named the islands of Leyte and Samar as Las Islas Filipinas. At the time, Philip was merely the prince of Asturias. (Over the next 300 years, the Spanish colonised the other islands that now make up the Philippines.)

33. **The 38th parallel**. The actual border now cuts across this circle of latitude but the name has stuck. At the end of the second world war, the Allies had to decide what to do with Japan's colony. A dividing line was proposed by America that extended far enough north to include Seoul and this was acceptable to the Soviet Union, which had troops in Korea long before the Americans arrived. After the Korean war the adversaries agreed to turn the frontline into the de facto border. Its proximity to the 38th parallel was no coincidence—the status quo had been restored.

34. The **Yalu** or **Amnok River**. The river, around 500 miles (805km) long, flows from the Tian Lake (known in Korean as Chon Lake) on Mount Baitou (Paektu) on the China–North Korea border to the Korean Bay.

35. **Shoes**. When she and her husband fled the Philippines as mass demonstrations against his rule gathered strength, airlifted from the presidential palace in Manila by American helicopter, they left their possessions behind. These included, by some accounts, 3,000 pairs of shoes

belonging to Imelda. Over 800 pairs have found their way to the museum. Many others have reportedly been attacked by termites and damaged by flooding while in storage.

36. **The Beach**. The novel, later filmed with Leonardo di Caprio in the lead role, was published in 1996 and is narrated by Richard, a young British traveller who acquires a map leading to a secluded beach, legendary among backpackers. But the community that lives there, seemingly in paradise, pays a high price for its existence.

37. **Kabul**. The British, who ruled India at the time, suspected that the Russian empire to the north had its eye on its prized colony. By conquering Afghanistan the British sought to stop a Russian invasion through the Khyber pass. British and Indian troops reached Kabul in April 1839 but resentment at their presence grew and the outnumbered British force negotiated a retreat to Jalalabad in India. But 4,500 British troops and 12,000 civilians who had followed the army to Kabul were all picked off in the mountain passes—part from Dr Brydon, who may have been allowed to live by the Afghans in order to tell the horrifying tale.

38. **Thailand**, **Laos** and **Myanmar**. The "golden triangle", where the Ruak River flows into the Mekong, is known as Sop Ruak locally. Its more familiar name is thought to have originated in America's State Department,

when it had its eye on the opium that emanated from the remote area. Now it is also known as a tourist spot.

39. **Mongolia**. There are less than two Mongolians per square kilometre. But there are other places where the neighbours may be farther away. In Greenland, which is administratively part of Denmark, there are just 0.1 people per square kilometre (0.26 people per square mile) and in the Falkland Islands, a possession of the United Kingdom, 0.2 people.

40. **Javan rhino**. The beast, whose distribution once extended from north-east India, through mainland south-east Asia, to the island of Sumatra, has a single horn of up to about 10 inches (254mm). Vietnam's last Javan rhino was killed by poachers in 2010 and now just 60 or so survive in the wild in Indonesia in the Ujung Kulon National Park.

41. **West**. The massive eruption of Krakatau, as the volcano is correctly known, is said to have killed 36,000 people. The sound of the explosion was reputedly heard 3,000 miles away and the ash thrown up affected global weather patterns for years. The producers are said to have stuck with "east" as it sounded better than west.

42. **Jindo**. Medium-sized and muscular and originally bred to hunt deer, rabbits and boars, the Jindo is also popular with dog aficionados outside South

Korea. The breed was officially recognised by the United Kingdom Kennel Club in 2005 and the American Kennel Club in 2008.

43. **Tamerlane**. Timur-i lang, or "Timur the Lame" as he was known by Europeans during the 16th century. His Turkic name was Timur, which means "iron". He was wounded while stealing sheep in his youth and was left lame in the right leg and with a stiff right arm for the rest of his life. From 1370 until his death in 1405, Timur built a powerful empire and was the last of the great nomadic leaders. His conquests were noted not only for their extent but also for their ferocity.

44. **Robert Louis Stevenson**. The Scottish author of *Treasure Island*, *Kidnapped* and *The Strange Case of Dr Jekyll and Mr Hyde* came to the South Pacific in 1888 to write about life on the islands and for the sake of his health. The tropical climate helped his tuberculosis and he decided to stay in Samoa where he built a mansion overlooking the sea. Sadly, despite the good weather, he died there at the age of 44 in 1894.

45. **Cox's Bazar**. Captain Hiram Cox was appointed as the superintendent of Palonki (today's Cox's Bazar) after Warren Hastings became the governor of Bengal. To commemorate his role in establishing the place as an important market town, it was named after him.

46. **Mount Pinatubo**. The volcano's apparent lack of activity had encouraged tens of thousands to make homes on its slopes and surrounding valleys. But it was not extinct and an earthquake the previous year seems to have triggered the eruption. Fortunately seismologists saw the eruption coming and thousands were evacuated from the surrounding area. Nevertheless, around 800 people lost their lives.

47. **Mohammad Ali Jinnah**. Jinnah, a lawyer based in Bombay (now Mumbai) and a believer in Hindu-Muslim unity, came to the conclusion that a homeland was the only way to safeguard the rights of Indian Muslims. Negotiations with the British government resulted in the partition of India and the formation of Pakistan in August 1947. But the birth of the new country came at the cost of violence and a vast movement of people between the new states in which hundreds of thousands died.

48. **India and Sri Lanka**. The strait, between 40 and 80 miles (64 and 128km) wide and around 85 miles long, connects the Bay of Bengal to the north-east with Palk Bay and the Gulf of Mannar to the south-west. It is peppered with islands and reefs that are known as Adam's Bridge. The port of Jaffna, northern Sri Lanka's main city, lies on the shore of the strait.

49. **Taipei, Taiwan**. With 101 storeys above ground and at a height of 1,671 feet (509 metres) the building formerly known as the Taipei World

Financial Centre surpassed the 1,483-foot Petronas Towers located in Kuala Lumpur. It held the record until 2010, with the opening of the Burj Khalifa in Dubai at 2,717 feet.

50. **Rhododendron**. *Rhodos* (rose) *dendron* (tree). The vast Rhododendron forests of Nepal attract thousands of trekkers when the plants are flowering in March and May. The Himalayas are home to the widest variety of species with Nepal alone home to over 30, where locals use the trees for traditional medicine, firewood and furniture and the flowers for food—though with care, as the plants can be highly toxic. Smaller species of rhododendrons are found elsewhere—in America it is the state flower of both West Virginia and Washington.

DRAGON'S DEN: China

1. **Five**. There are four smaller stars to the right of a larger one. The large star represents the Communist Party; the smaller stars the four classes of society: the working class, peasantry, petty bourgeoisie, and patriotic capitalists. Five is also an auspicious number in China.

2. **One**. Though roughly the size of America the country has a single zone based on Beijing time. It has not always been so. In 1912 China established five time zones but in 1949 Mao Zedong imposed a single one for the purposes of national unity. This can cause problems, particularly in far-flung Xinjiang, where the sun might set at midnight and rise mid-morning. The use of unofficial local time adds to the confusion.

3. **The sixth century** BCE. Kong Qui, better known in the west as Confucius, was born in 551 BCE near present-day Qufu. His aphorisms, written down after his death in the Analects, have been translated repeatedly. He died in 479 BCE but Confucianism later became the official imperial philosophy.

4. *The Art of War*. Though it is unclear who wrote the book and when or if Sun Tzu ever existed, military commanders and statesmen have followed its teachings for centuries. Napoleon is said to have read one of the first

translations into a western language. Mao Zedong credits it with helping him to defeat Chiang Kai-Shek's Nationalist forces. After Tony Soprano, a TV mobster, told his therapist he was reading the book it flew off the shelves once again.

5. **Xian**, **Nanjing** and **Luoyang**. Beijing means "northern capital" and has served that role for most of the past 600 years. Nanjing, meaning "southern capital", fulfilled the role from 200 CE to 1400. Xian, in the west, was a capital for much of the period between 1000 BCE and 1000 CE. Luoyang, now a small city in Henan province, was a capital for several periods between 500 BCE and 1000 CE. The list of capitals of different dynasties and governments has now expanded to around eight.

6. **The terracotta army**. Sometimes called the eighth wonder of the ancient world, the discovery of shards of pottery led to the unearthing of a pit containing 6,000 life-sized figures of soldiers. Excavation in 1976 uncovered two more pits both filled with terracotta warriors. In total the remains of nearly 8,000 terracotta figures have been recovered. The army guards the tomb of Qin Shi Huang Di, the first emperor of China, who died over 2,200 years ago.

7. **Marco Polo**. Polo and his parents, wealthy Venetian merchants, spent many years in the court of Kublai Khan. Polo acted as an emissary for the

Mongol ruler, at one stretch spending 17 years in his lands. He told his tales in several books including *Il Millione* and *The Travels of Marco Polo*, dictating some of them to a fellow prisoner in a Genoese jail.

8. **Chinese languages.** The Mandarin spoken in Beijing is the official national language of mainland China and is called Putonghua. Han Chinese make up about nine-tenths of the population and two-thirds of Han speak a variant of Mandarin. Cantonese is spoken in the south and Hong Kong. The other languages are spoken by much smaller numbers.

9. **The Temple of Heaven.** The buildings, set in gardens and surrounded by historic pine woods, form the most complete existing imperial sacrificial complex in China. The centrepiece, the Hall of Prayer for Good Harvests, is a magnificent triple-layered umbrella roof atop a three-tiered marble terrace. Wooden beams support the ceiling without the use of nails or cement.

 10. **Africa.** His fleet was much larger than anything the Europeans could manage at the time, with some ships 120 metres (400 feet) long. His first fleet contained 317 ships. But the Chinese did not use the voyages for conquest, more as a show of power. After Zheng He's death, the costly trips were abandoned, especially as the empire faced the threat of the Mongols in the north. By 1525, the empire ordered the destruction of all ocean-going ships.

11. **The Great Hall of the People**. The vast building is divided into three sections. The central part mainly includes the Great Auditorium and Central Hall. The northern section consists of the State Banquet Hall and the State Guest Hall and the southern part is an administrative building of the Standing Committee of the People's Congress of China. Each province, special administrative region and autonomous region of China has its own hall within the Great Hall, decked out in regional style.

12. **Potala Palace**. The winter residence of the Dalai Lama, made up of the White Palace, which contains the main ceremonial hall and throne of the Dalai Lama, and the Red Palace, is built on Red Mountain in the centre of Lhasa Valley. Norbulingka, the Dalai Lama's summer palace, constructed in the 18th century, is located on the bank of the Lhasa River about a mile west of the Potala.

13. **The Summer Palace**. Construction began on a royal garden and palace in 1750 on the orders of Emperor Qianglong and it had become the main residence for the royal family by the end of the Qing dynasty. Kunming Lake covers most of the area of the palace and gardens and is one of the few parts of the complex to survive the assault by an Anglo-French army in 1860 at the end of the second opium war.

14. **Hangzhou**. Construction began in the fifth century BCE on what was to become the world's longest man-made waterway. The canal, which also

connects five of the country's main river basins, was built to transport grain, rice and other raw material from rich agricultural lands to the cities of northern China. It is still in use today, carrying both goods and tourists.

15. **Yangtze**. Construction of the controversial dam displaced 1.4 million people and flooded 13 cities, 140 towns, and 1,350 villages with a reservoir more than 660km (410 miles) long. It has 32 sets of turbine generators, with a production capacity of 22.5 million kilowatts of electricity.

16. **Second opium war**. The first opium war (1839–42) was fought between China and Britain. For the second (1856–60), France joined in. The wars resulted from China's attempts to suppress the opium trade. Illegal imports began in the 18th century but expanded vastly in the next, resulting in widespread addiction. The second war was the result of the despatch of British and French troops to force China to sign trade treaties, including for opium.

17. **Hong Kong**. China ceded Hong Kong Island to Britain in 1842, at the end of the first opium war. China ceded the Kowloon Peninsula in 1860, ending the second opium war and then leased the New Territories to Britain in 1898 for 99 years.

18. **The Taiping rebellion**. Hong Xiuquan, from southern China, after failing the exams for imperial office for a third time, fell into a delirious state for a

month. This left him believing that he and his followers had been chosen to eject the Qing dynasty and rule China. The Taiping rebellion was a revolt by a peasant army, eventually numbering 100,000, that sought to create a classless society without private property. After initial success Hong was installed as emperor in Nanjing. The ensuing civil war lasted 14 years; around 20 million people lost their lives. Aided by Britain and the other western powers the Qing eventually defeated the Taiping rebels.

19. **The Boxer rebellion**. The uprising of northern Chinese peasants in red headscarves, called boxers by westerners because they performed physical exercises they believed would make them impervious to bullets, killed foreigners and Chinese Christians and destroyed foreign property. An invasion by an eight-nation allied force of western and Japanese troops was required to lift a 55-day siege of Beijing's legation quarter.

20. **Manchuria**, when it was occupied by the Japanese, who installed Pu Yi as Emperor of Manchukuo. After the war, he was captured by the Russians, who handed him over to the Communist government. Eventually he was pardoned and became a gardener, dying in 1967. His story was told in the Bertolucci film *The Last Emperor*.

21. **Kuomintang**. The National People's Party of China was established by Sun Yat Sen in 1912 and was led from 1925 to 1975 by Chiang Kai Shek. It was the ruling party in China from 1928 until it lost to Mao

Zedong's communists in China's civil war in 1949, after which it formed a government in exile in Taiwan.

22. **"Marco Polo Bridge Incident"**. Japan's quest to become a great power led to the annexation of Korea in 1895, after the first Sino-Japanese war, and the takeover of Manchuria in 1931. A Japanese military exercise at the bridge in 1935 escalated into a battle and both sides sent thousands of troops. Japan's military might prevailed and by 1937 Beijing and Shanghai had fallen. The war continued until it became a part of the second world war.

23. **Hunan**. He was born on December 26, 1893, in Shaoshan, the son of wealthy farmers, and trained as a teacher but in 1921 became a founding member of the Chinese Communist Party. At the end of the second world war, civil war broke out between the Nationalist Kuomintang and the Communists, who were victorious. Mao proclaimed the founding of the People's Republic of China in 1949. He died in September 1976.

24. **To kill sparrows**. Sparrows were deemed one of the four great pests, along with mosquitoes, rats and flies. The banging of pots and pans meant that the sparrows (which ate the grain) would be unable to rest and would die of sheer exhaustion. The bird was nearly driven to extinction, but the insects they ate thrived, including locusts, which consumed far more grain than sparrows ever did. The Great Leap Forward, designed to boost agriculture

and industry, was a disaster leading to between 30 million and 55 million deaths from famine.

25. **"The Gang of Four"**. The group of influential figures in China's Communist Party during the latter years of Mao Zedong's rule included Mao's wife, Jiang Qing. They rose to prominence during the Cultural Revolution (1966–76) and as Mao's health began to decline took control of parts of the government. The unrest caused by the Cultural Revolution led to a political struggle with reformers including Deng Xiaoping and Zhou Enlai. When Mao died in 1976, the Gang of Four attempted to take control of China, but his eventual successor, Hua Guofeng, had them arrested.

26. The **younger brother of Jesus Christ**. The rebellion sought the overthrow of the Manchu imperial dynasty and the conversion of Chinese people to Christianity. Total deaths during the rebellion have been conservatively estimated at 20 million–30 million.

27. **In 2047**. The territory, which had been under British rule since 1842, remains an important financial centre. Macau, which had been leased by the Portuguese, was handed back to China in 1999; famous for its casinos, it is the Chinese equivalent of Las Vegas.

28. Hainan. The island's beaches, palm trees and scenery have earned it the nickname "eastern Hawaii" and make Hainan one of the country's favourite domestic tourist destinations.

29. Inner Mongolia. Though Chifeng is the largest city, Hohhot is the capital of the region in northern China that borders both Mongolia and Russia.

30. Takla Makan. Also known as the "Place of Ruins" and "Sea of Death", the Takla Makan is one of the world's biggest sandy deserts. It is flanked by the Tien Shan mountains to the north, the Kunlun mountains to the south and the Pamirs to the west. The Silk Road caravan route connecting China with Central Asia and Europe skirted the northern and western fringes of the Takla Makan.

31. Afghanistan. China borders 14 countries. It runs alongside Afghanistan for just 47 miles (76km). Next comes Tajikistan at 257 miles and Laos at 262 miles.

32. Shanghai. Pudong, across the Huangpu River from the Bund, the city's riverside boulevard, is home to the Shanghai Stock Exchange and many of the city's most recognisable new buildings including the Oriental Pearl Tower, the Shanghai World Financial Centre and Shanghai Tower.

33. Guangzhou. The name derives from a folk tale that 2,000 years ago five deities rode to Guangzhou on rams carrying rice plants in their mouths. These were given to the inhabitants and despite the barren soil of the area there was never another famine. The deities returned to the sky and the rams turned to stone.

34. Guangzhou again. Formerly known as Canton, it is the capital of Guangdong province with a population of over 13 million people. Located on the Pearl River, it has a large port and is close to both Hong Kong and Macau. Food is important to local life and Guangzhou has the largest number of restaurants per head of any city in China.

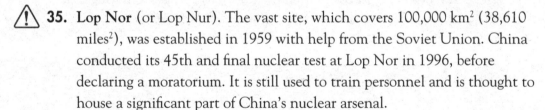 **35. Lop Nor** (or Lop Nur). The vast site, which covers 100,000 km^2 (38,610 miles^2), was established in 1959 with help from the Soviet Union. China conducted its 45th and final nuclear test at Lop Nor in 1996, before declaring a moratorium. It is still used to train personnel and is thought to house a significant part of China's nuclear arsenal.

36. Uighurs. Speaking a Turkic language and culturally closer to inhabitants of Central Asia, Uighurs complain that an influx of Han Chinese settlers over the past 50 years has made them a minority in their own land. Protests against discrimination have led to bloody clashes in the region. Uighurs claim that their cultural identity and way of life are under threat.

37. **Shih Tzu**. The small, fluffy dogs, given to members of the royal court as gifts by Tibet, were a favourite of Chinese rulers. The dowager empress Cixi, a dog lover, perfected the breed as it is known today but after her death in 1908 the royal kennels were destroyed and only a few dogs survived. Some made it to Britain and Norway where the breed was revived to become one of the most popular toy dogs in the world.

38. **Chow Chow** and **Shar-Pei**. The Chow Chow, originating in Mongolia and northern China, is one of the oldest dog breeds. Dogs resembling the Chow Chow appear in pottery and paintings of the Han dynasty (206 BCE–22 CE). One emperor reputedly kept 2,500 pairs as hunting dogs. The Shar-Pei, from southern China, is also believed by some to be an ancient breed. It may be this lineage that accounts for the blue tongues, but no one is quite sure.

39. **Richard Nixon**. The pandas were given to America after his historic visit in 1972 which ended a long diplomatic estrangement with the Communist regime. The pandas were a huge hit, receiving 1.1 million visitors in the first year. Nixon sent two musk oxen in return.

40. **Cormorants**. Though cormorant fishing is now mainly carried out to entertain tourists, for centuries birds have been trained to dive to catch fish and return to their owners. The birds are prevented from swallowing their prey by a ring placed around their neck.

41. Prawn. Legend has it that har gau were invented by the owner of a teahouse in Guangzhou at the start of the 19th century. Competition was intense so he bought fresh prawns readily available from the Pearl River, added pork and bamboo shoots and wrapped them in dumpling skins, to lure diners to his establishment.

42. Dog. Around 10,000 dogs are killed and eaten at the festival (which also celebrates a less divisive foodstuff, the lychee) despite widespread international outrage and a growing sense of disquiet in China itself.

43. The tea is rolled in **small pellets that resemble gunpowder** or lead shot. China is famed for its tea and once was the only producer known to the western world and the only source of tea imports. Lapsang Souchong, possibly the most famous Chinese tea, comes from the hills in north Fujian. Most gunpowder tea is produced in Pingshui in Zheijian province.

44. Sorghum. China's national drink, hailed for helping the Red Army survive the Long March, is mainly distilled from sorghum, although wheat, barley, millet or glutinous rice are also used. It is said to have originated in Sichuan in western China centuries ago and is a vital accompaniment to any toast, much to the chagrin of western businessmen who have struggled to come to terms with its strong flavour but glug it back anyway for fear of blowing big deals.

45. Didi Chuxing. The Chinese ride-hailing giant, which lets customers book a taxi at the touch of a smartphone, has been growing fast. Uber and Didi were in an intense fight until last year when the Chinese firm bought the American rival business in China. The company is valued at over $50 billion.

46. Taikonauts. The name is derived from *taikong*, the Chinese word for space. China's space programme dates back to the 1960s but the first person launched into space was Yang Liwei in 2003 aboard *Shenzhou 5*. China thus became the third country after the United States and Russia to send a man into orbit.

47. They are all soccer teams that played in the **Chinese Super League** in the 2017 season. The top flight of Chinese soccer was established in 2004 with 12 teams though it has now been expanded to 16. In recent years Chinese teams have paid huge sums to attract big names from the west including players such as Carlos Tevez and Oscar.

48. Ai Weiwei. Mr Ai, perhaps China's best-known artist beyond its shores, has long fallen foul of China's authorities for his outspoken criticism of the government and its repression of free speech. He was detained for 81 days in 2011 during a crackdown on political dissent and banned from travelling abroad for over four years.

49. *Raise the Red Lantern*. The film made an international star of Gong Li, already famous in China for her roles in *Red Sorghum* and *Ju Dou*. In the film she portrays a young woman confined in a huge mansion with three other wives who conspire against the youthful and pretty interloper. The red lantern hangs outside the rooms of the wife the old man favours.

50. *Private Lives*. The art-deco gem was opened in 1929 and drew the rich and famous from all over the world. The hotel was widely known as the "Number One mansion in the Far East", because of its location on a corner of the Bund, Shanghai's waterfront promenade, and Nanjing Road, with its shops and nightlife. Famous guests included Charlie Chaplin and George Bernard Shaw.

NATIONAL INQUIRERS: International

1. **United States** (89), **Switzerland** (46), **Iraq** (34), **Germany** (30), **New Zealand** (23), **Russia** (9).

2. 72, according to the International Lesbian, Gay, Bisexual, Trans and Intersex Association. In 45 of these, the law is applied to women as well as men.

3. 192. Members include South Sudan and Timor-Leste but exclude Kosovo and Palestine.

4. **Pakistan**, **Jordan**, **Turkey**, **Cyprus**, **Egypt**, **Iran** and **Israel**; scientists from these seven countries, not known for their close collaboration as a general rule, have worked together on the particle accelerator in Jordan.

5. **Judaism**. It also has the smallest gender gap.

6. **Islam**, which is predicted to grow by 70%—twice as fast as the overall world population. In the second half of this century it is expected to surpass Christianity as the world's largest religious group.

7. The **Holy See** and the **State of Palestine**. Non-member states have been granted observer status 16 times in the past—usually because of the veto of one of the permanent members of the security council.

8. **Syria, Afghanistan** and **Iraq**. There were 1.2 million asylum applications in 2016, down slightly from 1.3 million in 2015, although some of the applicants may have applied for asylum in multiple countries. Germany received almost half of all applications.

9. **Sweden**, a relic of its policy of neutrality in armed conflicts. It does, however, participate in NATO exercises.

10. **International child abduction**. The 1980 treaty requires countries to send abducted children back to the jurisdiction of where they have been living previously. It is an important treaty in determining the rules of international adoption.

11. **10.3 million**, as of 2017. Apart from the Seychelles, America imprisons the highest number of people compared to the size of its population.

12. **11%**, according to the modern yardstick for destitution: that a person consumes less than $1.90 a day at 2011 purchasing-power parity. That is down from 42% who were defined as being extremely poor in 1981.

13. **Central African Republic, Congo, Mali, Sudan's Darfur region** and **South Sudan**.

14. **775**; in June 2017, 41 were still imprisoned there.

15. Any of **Argentina, Australia, Belgium, Bolivia, Brazil, Costa Rica, Democratic Republic of Congo, Dominican Republic, Ecuador, Egypt, Greece, Honduras, Lebanon, Luxembourg, Mexico, Nauru, Panama, Paraguay, Peru, Singapore, Thailand** or **Uruguay**.

16. **About a quarter**. The rate is slightly lower today than it was in the 1990s.

17. **Trygve Lie** (Norway), **Dag Hammarskjöld** (Sweden), **U Thant** (Myanmar), **Kurt Waldheim** (Austria), **Javier Pérez de Cuellar** (Peru), **Boutros Boutros-Ghali** (Egypt), **Kofi Annan** (Ghana), **Ban Ki-moon** (Korea), **António Guterres** (Portugal).

18. **China, Russia, Japan, Switzerland, Britain, Italy**. The rates range from almost ten marriages per 1,000 people at the top end to less than four at the bottom.

19. **"Well below" 2°C above pre-industrial levels**. Given that the world has already warmed by approximately 1.2°C, this is hugely ambitious.

20. In all of those countries but Russia, **the share is more than 10%**, and in all but Russia the numbers grew between 2000 and 2015. In Russia the proportion has remained the same.

21. 14. All have been scaled and the tallest, Mount Everest, has been climbed more than 7,000 times.

22. **Seven years old.** The United Nations Committee on the Rights of the Child recommended an "absolute minimum" age of 12 for criminal responsibility.

23. **That of the Commonwealth of Dominica.** For an investment of $100,000 plus fees and an interview, you can buy citizenship of the small Caribbean island.

24. a) **1945** b) **1948** c) **1995**.

25. c) **Brazil.**

26. **They are all from countries in Africa.** As of 2017, other investigations were under way in countries such as Afghanistan, Georgia and Iraq, but no one has been indicted yet.

27. **About a fifth**, according to estimates by the World Health Organization in 2015. That figure is down from a quarter ten years earlier. But among men in Africa and the eastern Mediterranean, rates are going up.

28. It gave Saddam Hussein a final chance to **comply with weapons inspections** and was used to justify legally the launching of military action against Saddam Hussein in 2003.

 29. **Two-fifths**. In half of those countries, the time served by female leaders falls short of five years, the common length of a full single term in office.

30. **Estonia**, where mothers can stay at home for three years, receiving about a year and a half's salary. The most generous countries are generally in Central and Eastern Europe, where governments spooked by rapidly shrinking populations are trying to encourage couples to have more babies.

31. **The longest speech given** at the United Nations General Assembly. The UN delegates should have counted themselves lucky: he spoke for 7 hours and 10 minutes at the 1986 Communist party congress in Havana.

32. **In 1980**, after a global immunisation campaign led by the World Health Organization. The last known case was in Somalia in 1977.

33. **Honduras**, **El Salvador** and **Venezuela**. Their latest murder rates per 100,000 population were 74.6, 64.2 and 62 respectively.

34. **4%**, according to research by two neurosurgeons. Many non-specialist sites, such as Tumblr, also provide erotic images.

35. **A little over half** (54%), up from a third in 1960. The share of urbanites continues to grow.

36. They are **Caesarean sections**. In Brazil's private health-care system, they account for nearly nine in ten births.

37. a) **New York** b) **the Hague** c) **Paris** d) **Seattle**.

38. **None**, because no such guidelines exist. Less than half of countries offer fathers any leave at all.

39. **0.7% of gross national income**. In 2015 just six rich countries—Britain, Denmark, Luxembourg, the Netherlands, Norway and Sweden—met the goal.

40. a) **Athens** b) **Berlin** c) **Munich** d) **Barcelona**.

41. The **19th century** (bonus point for getting the year: **1815**) in **Indonesia** when **Mount Tambora**, a volcano, erupted. Between 60,000 and 120,000 people were killed by the ash flows, the tsunamis and the starvation that followed. The effect on the global climate was such that 1816 was dubbed "the year without a summer".

42. **About a quarter** (26%). Such laws are most common in the Middle East and North Africa. Apostasy laws exist only there and in Asia and sub-Saharan Africa but blasphemy laws can be found in all regions.

43. The world average for those born between 2000 and 2015 is **71 years**; the **Japanese** have the longest life expectancy (83.7 years) while those in **Sierra Leone** have the shortest (50.1 years). Average life expectancy is, in general, rising rapidly; it increased by more over the past four generations than over the previous 8,000.

44. **Yasser Arafat**, **Yitzhak Rabin** and **Shimon Peres** won it in 1994 for their efforts to bring about peace in the Middle East. **Ellen Johnson Sirleaf**, **Leymah Gbowee** and **Tawakkul Karman** won it in 2011 for their non-violent struggle for women's rights.

45. **Estonia**. It is not a route to citizenship but rather a form of digital identity. The first recipient was Edward Lucas, an *Economist* journalist.

46. **America**, **New Zealand** and **Ukraine**. New Zealand has also become a hot spot for the development of "legal highs" since conventional drugs

traffickers have little interest in serving 4 million people far out in the South Pacific.

47. **Sweden**, in the late 1950s, when it televised debates between the party leaders. America held its first televised presidential debate in 1960 between John F. Kennedy and Richard Nixon. Nixon's sweaty appearance is thought to have damaged his prospects among viewers.

48. How close the world is to **catastrophic disaster**, taking into account such risks as climate change and the possible use of nuclear weapons. It was invented by the *Bulletin of the Atomic Scientists*. It is currently set at two and a half minutes to midnight. In 1953, after America had tested its first thermonuclear device and the Soviets tested their own H-bomb, it was set to two minutes to midnight.

49. **Childhood obesity**. The number of children aged 0–5 who were overweight rose by a third between 1990 and 2013. This is forecast to soar by another 70% by 2025 if nothing is done.

50. **Africa**, according to research by the World Health Organization, with 26.9 fatalities for every 100,000 people in 2013 compared with 9.3 in Europe— which has ten times more cars per head of population.

FIRM FAVOURITES: Business

1. **Apple**. The company's name was inspired by Steve Job's fruitarian diet and a visit to an apple farm. Many myths surround the current logo, an Apple with a bite taken out of it, including that it is a reference to the suicide of Alan Turing using a poisoned apple or to Adam and Eve. The truth is more prosaic. According to its designer the bite is for scale, to avoid confusion with a cherry.

2. **Subaru**. The Japanese carmaker is a division of Fuji Heavy Industries. The large star is said to represent FHI and the five smaller ones the companies that came together in 1953 to form the larger firm. There are only six stars in the logo because two of the seven stars of the constellation are too close together to distinguish with the naked eye.

3. **Mazda**. The name is derived from Ahura-Mazda, a Zoroastrian deity associated with wisdom. The firm's founder, Jujiro Matsuda, was deeply spiritual but may have also been influenced by the mangled western pronunciations of his name.

4. **Adidas** and **Puma**. The reason for the enmity between Adolf ("Adi") Dassler and his brother, Rudolf, is unclear. But it led to the break-up of

Gebrüder Dassler Schuhfabrik and the founding of the two sportswear brands. The headquarters of the two firms still stand on opposite banks of the river Aurach in Herzogenaurach, a small town in southern Germany.

5. **Google**. In 1996, Larry Page and Sergey Brin called their search-engine program BackRub to emphasise the importance of a website's "back links", the number of links from other sites. Later the pair took a fancy to Googol, 1 followed by 100 zeroes, after a brainstorming session. The term was mistyped when checking if the domain name was free and Google stuck instead.

6. **Shells**. Importing shells from the Far East laid the foundations for an import and export business that sent machinery, textiles and tools to newly industrialising Japan and the Far East and brought back rice, silk, china and copperware to the Middle East and Europe. An interest in oil developed during a trip to Azerbaijan. Petroleum was also produced in the East Indies, a Dutch colony, by the Royal Dutch Petroleum Company, which merged with Shell in 1907.

7. **Apple** used this slogan from 1997 to 2002, causing millions of purists to wince and mutter "Think Differently" under their breaths.

8. **De Beers**. Created for the diamond mining firm in 1947 by the NW Ayer agency, the campaign was also supposedly responsible for inventing the idea

of the diamond engagement ring, which was not the accepted way to seal a proposal of marriage before that time.

9. **United Airlines**. Created by Leo Burnett in 1965, the airline dropped the tagline in 1996. It was revived in 2013 but four years later the phrase was used to ridicule United after it dragged a paying passenger off one of its overbooked flights.

10. **Burger King**. BBDO came up with the phrase in 1973 and it was used widely for decades. In 2014 the company partly revived the idea with a new tagline: "Be Your Way".

11. **Volkswagen**. Doyle Dane Bernbach (DDB) came up with the phrase in 1959 to convince Americans to end their love affair with the vast gas guzzlers made in Detroit and choose a small German car, the Beetle, instead.

12. **Avis**. The slogan came from DDB in 1962, as the car-hire firm, perennially second to Hertz, was attempting to reverse several years of losses. It seemed to work, returning the company to profit. The slogan was dropped in 2012 in favour of "It's Your Space".

13. **James Cash Penney**. The American department store magnate set up his first shop with two partners in Kemmerer, Wyoming, in 1902. The firm now has over 1,000 outlets across America.

14. **Frank Winfield Woolworth**. The first Woolworth store was opened in Utica, New York, in 1878. The name still survives in Austria, Germany and Mexico. The FootLocker chain of sporting goods stores is a direct descendant.

15. **Leon Leonwood Bean**. Founded in 1912 in Freeport, Maine, the clothing firm's headquarters are a short walk from the company's original shop.

16. The label was founded in Los Angeles in 1962 by **Herb Alpert** (a trumpet player who also found fame with The Tijuana Brass) and **Jerry Moss**. The company was one of the world's biggest independent record companies and boasted the Carpenters, The Police and Bryan Adams among the stars on its label. It eventually became part of Polygram in 1989 and then Universal Music in 1998.

17. From **Joseph Cyril Bamford**. The giant construction-equipment firm was founded in 1945 to build agricultural tipping trailers and is still owned by members of the Bamford family.

18. **Ingvar Kamprad**'s initials have been added to the initial of the farm where he grew up, **Elmtaryd**, and the village he calls home, **Agunnaryd**. Have a mark if you got Ingvar Kamprad, who founded the firm in 1943 as a mail-order business and began to sell furniture five years later.

19. Forrest **Mars** and William Bruce **Murrie**. Forrest Mars, a member of the family confectionery firm, copied the idea when he saw British soldiers eating Smarties, chocolate covered in a hard sugar coating that did not melt in the heat, during the Spanish civil war. Murrie became involved because he was part of the Hershey family, which controlled chocolate rationing during the war.

20. **Louis Vuitton Moët Hennessey**. Louis Vuitton founded his luggage company in Paris in 1854. Claude Moët began making champagne in 1743 and was joined by Pierre-Gabriel Chandon in 1833. The Cognac firm was founded by Richard Hennessy in 1765 and joined forces with Moët in 1971. The firm was formed when the two companies merged again in 1987 and is now the world's biggest luxury-goods company with some 70 brands including Dior and Givenchy.

21. **Yahoo.** The species was described as filthy and unpleasant and the term later came to be used for loutish behaviour. But the company's name also in part derives from the acronym for "Yet Another Hierarchical Officious Oracle".

22. **International Business Machines**. Nicknamed "Big Blue", the IT and consulting firm was incorporated in 1911 as the Computing Tabulating Recording Company, but its origins go back to the end of the 19th century.

23. **Bayerische Motoren Werke**. The firm was founded in 1916 to construct aero-engines and started making cars only in 1928 under licence from Britain's Austin. It began designing its own cars in 1932.

24. **Fabbrica Italiana Automobili Torino**. The company was founded in 1899 and a year later opened its first factory from which emerged 24 cars a year. Fiat, under the Agnelli family, eventually went on to own Ferrari, Maserati and Lancia. In 2014 Fiat and the American carmaker Chrysler merged to form FCA.

25. **Minnesota Mining** and **Manufacturing**. The company was founded in 1902 to mine corundum. Though this venture was largely unsuccessful, the company turned to other materials and other products. In 1925 a young technician invented "Scotch" masking tape and in 1980 it introduced Post-It notes, adding to the range of products it makes today for a wide variety of applications.

26. **Lucky Goldstar**. The South Korean conglomerate was formed in 1958 through the merger of two Korean companies, Lak-Hui (pronounced "Lucky") and GoldStar. The former sold household goods while Goldstar

made electronic products such as radios, TVs, fridges, washing machines and air conditioners. The corporate name was change to LG in 1995. The slogan "Life's Good" is a "backronym".

27. **Niki Lauda**. Lauda came out of retirement in 1982 and went on to win the championship again in 1984. Lauda Air became a subsidiary of Austrian Airlines in 2000, which retained the branding on planes until 2013.

28. **Salvador Dali**. Despite painting melting clocks and keeping a pet ocelot called Babou, the most surreal act of the famous Spanish artist may well be his association with Chupa Chups. He designed the logo in 1969 for his friend and the founder of the company, Enric Bernat, while the pair ate lunch at a restaurant.

29. **Pierce & Pierce**. Bateman is a specialist in mergers and acquisitions at the fictional firm. Sherman McCoy, the "master of the universe" in Tom Wolfe's novel *Bonfire of the Vanities*, worked at the same firm.

30. *Up in the Air*. Many of those fired by the corporate downsizing expert in the film, released in 2009, are not actors but people who had been recently laid off work.

⚠ 31. **Tyrell Corporation**. The film is adapted from Philip K. Dick's novel of 1968, *Do Androids Dream of Electric Sheep?* In fact, it is left somewhat ambiguous whether Deckard is an android though the director subsequently insisted that he was.

32. *2001: A Space Odyssey*. In Stanley Kubrick's sci-fi epic, based on the novel by Arthur C. Clarke, HAL, a sentient computer, tries to kill the crew of a spacecraft on route to Jupiter after they question the purpose of the mission. Artificial intelligence cheerleaders take note.

33. **Oceanic Airlines**. The name has turned up repeatedly in film and television, most famously in *Lost*. The crash of Oceanic flight 815 on a mysterious island was the start of six seasons of entertaining bafflement for viewers.

34. **Croydon**. The airport's origins go back to the first world war, when the Royal Flying Corps were stationed at Beddington to intercept Zeppelins attacking London. In 1920 London's airport was moved from a temporary aerodrome on Hounslow Heath to Croydon. Croydon to Paris became the world's busiest air route.

35. **Le Bourget**. The airport, opened in 1919, was the spot where Charles Lindbergh landed in *Spirit of St. Louis* after the first solo transatlantic flight in 1927. It now serves business jets and is home to the Paris Air Show, one of the world's biggest aviation get-togethers.

36. **Andy Warhol**. The American pop artist began his career as a commercial artist working for magazines but in the early 1960s began making art based on mass-produced images from American popular culture. By some estimates his estate was worth $510 million at the time of his death in 1987.

37. **Calvin Coolidge**. He made his famous remark in an address to the Society of American Newspaper Editors in Washington, DC, in 1925. On hearing of the death of the famously reserved president, nicknamed "Silent Cal", Dorothy Parker, a renowned American wit, is reported to have remarked, "How can they tell?"

38. **Warren Buffett**. Mr Buffett, nicknamed the "sage of Omaha", is one of the most successful investors of all time. Berkshire Hathaway, his investment firm, owns or has big stakes in many well-known firms including Netjets, Kraft Heinz and Coca-Cola.

39. **Winston Churchill**. Britain's wartime prime minister had a seemingly insatiable appetite for cigars and champagne. He was also a prolific author, partly because he often faced large debts from the cost of his high-living lifestyle.

40. **America**. The United States leads the pack, accounting for around a fifth of total world output, closely followed by Russia.

41. Russia. Russia and Saudi Arabia have swapped places in recent years. America is in third place.

42. China. The country is by far the world's biggest producer of coal, followed by America, India and Australia.

43. Czech Republic. According to Kirin, a Japanese brewer, Czechs drank 142.4 litres per head in 2015, the equivalent of 250 pints. Fortunately Czech brewers make cheap and excellent beer.

44. L'Oréal. In 1907 Eugène Schueller, the company's founder, was the first person to sell synthetic hair dye. He called his new product Auréole. Liliane Bettencourt, L'Oréal's main shareholder, is said to be the world's richest woman.

45. Comcast. The American firm is the world's biggest media and TV company by revenue. It was founded in Tupelo, Mississippi, in 1963 as a cable TV firm with 1,200 subscribers.

46. Intel. The world's biggest chipmaker was founded in 1968 and its name is a contraction of Integrated Electronics.

47. Google. Larry Page met Sergey Brin for the first time when he went to Stanford University as a prospective PhD student. Brin was his tour guide.

48. **Alibaba**. Mr Ma founded China's answer to Amazon in 1999 after two previous internet ventures failed. Its IPO in 2014 was the world's biggest public stock offering and it has made Mr Ma China's richest man.

49. **Uber**. The ride-hailing firm, founded in 2009, now operates in early 600 cities around the world, is hated by cab drivers and is so large and successful that it has, like Google, become a verb—to "Uber it". Mr Kalanick resigned as chief executive in June 2017.

50. The *Washington Post*. Mr Bezos, who vies with Bill Gates as the world's richest man, bought the paper for $250 million in 2013.

CAPITAL BRAINS: Finance and economics

1. **Ancient Greek**, in which the term referred to the management of a household or estate.

2. **Thomas Carlyle**, the 19th-century historian. He used the phrase in a book arguing for the reintroduction of slavery.

3. The 300th anniversary of **Sweden's Riksbank**, the world's first central bank. Its official name is the "Swedish National Bank's Prize in Economic Sciences in memory of Alfred Nobel" and some people sniff that it is not a "real" Nobel prize. But winners receive their prize at the same ceremony as other Nobel laureates (apart from the peace prize).

4. **Elinor Ostrom in 2009**. Her work was on the management of collective resources. Only around a quarter of economics undergraduates in Britain are women.

5. **Mathematics**. Although he received a first class degree, he only finished 12th in the university for maths; he was used to being top.

6. a) **John Maynard Keynes** b) **Milton Friedman** c) **Paul Krugman** d) **Paul Samuelson**.

7. The phrase, according to *Merriam-Webster*, dates back to the early 19th century and relates to the use of water to try to get a pump working again, when blocked with air. In economic terms, it dates at least to the 1920s; **a little stimulus can generate a lot more activity**. It was not coined by Donald Trump, as he claimed in an interview with *The Economist*.

8. a) **Sir Thomas Gresham**, a financier in the Tudor era. The idea stems from a time when coins were made up of gold and silver. In theory, their metallic value was equal to their purchasing power; a pound coin was a pound's worth of silver. But many coins were debased. So consumers will use the debased coins to buy goods and keep the pure coins; over time, only debased (bad) money will circulate. b) **Jean-Baptiste Say**, a French economist. When a good or service is sold, the revenue raised goes back into the economy as wages or profits. Those who receive the wages and profits thus have the money to buy other goods and services; there cannot be a general glut. c) **Charles Goodhart**, a British economist, first suggested this in 1975. The idea was used to criticise the money supply growth targets that were a key part of monetarism. Awareness of the target may cause individuals to alter their behaviour; as a result the given measure may no longer be a useful indicator.

9. a) **Purchasing power parity**—a measure of comparing standards of living across countries b) **foreign direct investment**—when foreign investors set up factories in a country (if they just buy shares, that's portfolio investment) c) **purchasing managers index**—a measure of business sentiment.

10. a) **David Ricardo**—the consequence of this insight is that it is worthwhile for two countries to trade even if one is more efficient at producing all products than the other. b) **Eli Heckscher** and **Bertil Ohlin** c) **William Jevons, Léon Walras** and **Carl Menger** had the insight that the utility of each additional item to the consumer declines with quantity; owning a single car is very useful, but it is less useful for someone with 19 cars to buy a 20th.

11. **Psychology**. Mr Kahneman, along with former colleague Amos Tversky, established the field of behavioural economics, which studies how psychological quirks affect our behaviour.

12. **Richard Thaler** of the University of Chicago. He explained the workings of synthetic collateralised debt obligations. It was a lot more entertaining than it sounds.

13. **Angus Maddison**. He estimated that the global economy has grown 500-fold since the start of the common era (CE 1 or AD 1).

14. a) **Earnings before interest tax, depreciation and amortisation**
b) **cyclically adjusted price-earnings ratio** c) **residential mortgage-backed securities**. The first is a core measure of the profits produced by individual companies; the second a method for valuing the overall stockmarket, based on averaging profits over 10 years; and the third are bonds, backed by home loans—the securities at the heart of the 2007–08 crisis.

15. a) **Luxembourg** at around $100,000 per head. The United States may be the biggest economy but some smaller countries are richer in individual terms. b) **Burundi**, at only $277. Sadly, the 14 poorest countries are all in Africa.

16. a) **Ukraine** and b) the **Comoros**. The standard measure is the Gini coefficient, which looks at the distribution of income; a figure of 1 means that all the income belongs to a single individual. European countries with their welfare states tend to be more equal, developing countries less so.

17. 8% and 7% respectively. Mutual funds carry charges and the index doesn't, so it is very hard for the average mutual fund to beat the index, as the index represents the performance of the average investor.

18. a) **John Pierpont**, the founder of the group who dominated the American financial system in the late 19th and early 20th centuries. After he organised a rescue of the banks in 1907, politicians decided that a US central bank was needed b) **Internationale Nederlanden Groep** or International Netherlands Group, a Dutch bank c) **Banco Bilbao Vizcaya Argentaria**, a Spanish bank.

 19. **Montagu Norman**, governor of the Bank of England from 1920 to 1944. A notable eccentric, he wore a broad-brimmed hat and flowing cape and suffered from regular nervous breakdowns. He liked to travel incognito on ocean liners.

20. a) **Alan Greenspan** b) **William McChesney Martin** c) **Paul Volcker**.

21. a) **Alan Greenspan** b) **Paul Volcker** c) **William McChesney Martin**.

22. **RJR Nabisco**, a tobacco and food conglomerate, which was one of the biggest targets of the leveraged buyout boom of the late 1980s. The firm was bought by the private equity group Kohlberg Kravis Roberts for $25 billion.

23. **Benjamin Graham**. Graham was the founding father of security analysis, writing classic books such as *The Intelligent Investor* and (along with David Dodd) *Security Analysis*. He pioneered the examination of balance sheets and value investing. Buffett studied under him at Columbia University and worked for his investment firm, Graham-Newman.

24. **Technical analysis**, or **Chartism**—the belief that past price movements predict future changes. The academic evidence for this is sketchy but there are plenty of people who follow the precepts.

25. **Because it contained tallow or beef fat.** This made the notes unacceptable to Hindus, vegans and others. The £10 note featuring Jane Austen is due to contain the same ingredient, but the Bank says it would cost too much to replace it. The Bank hopes that palm oil or coconut oil can be used in the £20 polymer note, due in 2020.

26. a) **Morgan Stanley** b) **Visa** c) **American Express**.

27. A **mountain resort** in New Hampshire in the United States.

28. **John Maynard Keynes** and **Harry Dexter White**. After the latter's death, it was revealed he had passed information to the Soviet Union.

29. The **International Monetary Fund** and the **World Bank**.

 30. A **fixed exchange rate, free capital mobility** and **monetary autonomy** (the ability to set interest rates independently). A country cannot have all three.

31. **The United States**. As of 2018, the person in charge is Jim Yong Kim.

32. **France.** As of early 2018, Christine Lagarde, a former French finance minister, holds the post.

33. a) **India** b) **Spain** c) **South Korea** d) **Brazil**.

34. a) **Mongolia** b) **Vietnam** c) **Honduras** d) **Paraguay**.

35. a) **Rome** b) **Lithuania** c) **Athens**.

 36. 78%. Most people rarely use high-denomination bills, but they are widely held by those operating in the black economy: drug traders or simply small businesses evading tax. In other countries the proportion is even higher—in Thailand, China, Japan and Argentina, the proportion of cash held in the highest-denomination bill is more than 80%.

37. a) **Equity Capital Markets** b) **Debt Capital Markets** c) **Fixed Income, Currencies and Commodities**.

38. **Basle,** or Basel, in Switzerland. The BIS is best known these days for its regular reports on the health of the financial system and the global economy.

39. a) **1995** b) **Geneva**.

40. These are **terms from the commodity market**, where materials like cotton and oil can be bought immediately (spot) or sold at a later date (future). Contango occurs when the futures price is higher than the spot price; backwardation when the futures price is lower.

41. It ran to **848 pages**. At the time of writing, the Trump administration is planning to repeal large parts of it.

42. 37. Those were the days.

43. R is the **rate of return on capital** and g is the **growth rate** of the economy. The idea is that if investment returns are higher than the growth rate, the rich will keep getting richer.

44. a) **Edwin Lefèvre** b) **Charles P. Kindleberger** c) **Fred Schwed Jr.**

45. *Lombard Street: A Description of the Money Market.* He believed that the central bank should lend freely in a crisis, but only against good collateral and at a high interest rate.

46. **BB or below** for Standard & Poor's and **Ba or below** for Moody's.

47. **Postal reply coupons**, which in theory could be bought cheaply in Europe and sold at a profit in the United States. In reality, Ponzi, like Bernie Madoff, paid off existing clients with the money he got from new clients.

48. It is a **fund**, or **annuity**, where all the **proceeds go to the last survivor**. Hence the temptation to commit murder.

49. **Robert Merton** and **Myron Scholes**.

50. a) **Long-Term Capital Management**; the author was Roger Lowenstein b) **Enron**; the authors were Bethany McLean and Peter Elkind c) **Bear Stearns**; the author was William Cohan.

TURING TEST: Science and technology

1. **Tin**, atomic number 50, is one of seven metallic elements known to the ancients (the others were iron, lead, gold, silver, copper and mercury). Being familiar materials, they tend to have short names, regardless of language. In English, though, tin has the shortest.

2. **Rutherfordium**; named after Ernest, Lord Rutherford, who discovered the atomic nucleus. Rutherfordium, atomic number 104, is a manmade element with a half-life of 1.3 hours.

3. **Yttrium**, **ytterbium**, **terbium** and **erbium**, atomic numbers 39, 70, 65 and 68. The village is Ytterby, 20km north-east of Stockholm, which is the site of a former mine that yielded all four, and also several other so-called rare earth metals, much prized for their electronic properties.

4. 11: hydrogen, nitrogen, oxygen, fluorine, chlorine, helium, neon, argon, krypton, xenon and radon. The first five on the list were discovered early in the history of chemistry, in the decades just before and after 1800. The last five, known as noble gases because they are chemically unreactive, were discovered in the 1890s and 1900s. Helium, also a noble gas, was identified

in 1868, by analysing the sun's spectrum, 27 years before it was isolated on Earth.

5. The **order of star classes**, ranked by temperature, in the main sequence of the Hertzsprung-Russell diagram. Each letter in the mnemonic corresponds to a star class. O- and B-class stars are the hottest and shortest lived. M-class stars are red dwarfs, the coolest and longest lived. The sun is in the middle, in class G.

6. **Ceres**, the largest member of the asteroid belt between Mars and Jupiter. When found, it was classified as a planet, because it appeared to be a missing object predicted by the Titus-Bode law of orbital radii. The discovery of other asteroids put paid to that idea.

7. **The Crab Nebula**. This is the remnant of a supernova observed by Chinese astronomers in 1054 CE. It is also the first item in Charles Messier's catalogue of nebulae (hence, M1), assembled in the 18th century. Messier was a comet-hunter and his catalogue was of objects that might have been mistaken for comets when observed through contemporary telescopes.

8. **Argon**. The first noble gas to be isolated, which was done in 1894 by William Ramsay who found that, after he had reacted nitrogen from the air with hot magnesium, a small amount of unreactive gas was left over.

9. **DEOXY**, as in deoxyribose nucleic acid. One of the chemical differences between RNA and DNA is that the sugar, ribose, which forms part of the former, has to lose an oxygen atom to form part of the latter.

10. **Barnacles**. He wrote four books about them between 1851 and 1854.

11. **Blue**. Really. It is not colourless. Vibration of its chemical bonds absorbs red light, leaving blue behind.

12. **A quark**. Quarks are fundamental particles that, because the interaction between them gets stronger as they separate, can never be isolated. Up and down quarks are the building blocks of protons and neutrons, and hence of atomic nuclei. The others are components of more exotic objects, produced in particle accelerators.

13. **In the brain**. In Greek, "sea horse" is "hippocampus". Deep inside each hemisphere of the brain is a structure that early anatomists thought resembled this peculiar fish. They are involved in long-term memory formation.

14. **In the pancreas**. They are clusters of cells, named after the anatomist who discovered them, that secrete insulin. Type-1 diabetes is a result of the sufferer's own immune system attacking them.

15. **Francis Crick**, in his paper with James Watson, describing the structure of DNA. He added the sentence at the last minute, though it stated the obvious, to make sure no one else claimed credit for realising the significance of DNA's double-helical structure.

16. **The presence of a nucleus**. Eukaryotes are plants, animals and fungi (and also a lot of single-celled critters such as amoebae). Prokaryotes are bacteria and archaea, a bacteria-like group recognised as distinct in 1977.

17. **Corundum**, of which sapphire and ruby are gem varieties. The numbers are mineral hardness on the Mohs scale. A higher number can scratch a lower one. The scale goes up to 10, which is diamond.

18. **Sagittarius**. That is why the Milky Way is brightest there. A powerful radio source called Sagittarius A* is believed to be a supermassive black hole at the galaxy's very centre.

19. **The Andromeda nebula**. This galaxy, M31 in Charles Messier's catalogue, is 2.5 million light years away and clearly visible to the naked eye if the sky is cloudless and there is no light pollution. A second galaxy, the Triangulum nebula, M33, which is 3 million light years away, can sometimes be seen with the naked eye, too, but was originally discovered by telescope.

20. **Celtic tribes that lived in Wales**. Much of the geological time scale was worked out by British geologists, which also explains the Cambrian (from Cambria, the Roman name for Wales) and the Devonian (from the county of Devonshire).

21. Around **4.54 billion years** old. An early calculation of about 6,000 years, based on Biblical data, turned out to be an underestimate. The modern figure uses rates of decay of radioactive elements to date meteorites that have remained unchanged since the beginning of the solar system, when Earth (the rocks of which have changed a lot) was formed.

22. Around **13.8 billion years** old. This estimate is based on data collected by the Planck space observatory, which can see directly back to within 380,000 years of the beginning of time. Before this, space was opaque.

23. **In a cell**. It is a complex of membranes that acts as a finishing shop for proteins.

24. **That the speed of light is invariant**. This was the crucial discovery upon which the theory of relativity was built. If the speed of light cannot vary, then space and time have to vary instead, to accommodate that fact.

25. **The Cretaceous**, that is, the period immediately following the Jurassic. Odd. But true.

26. **Brownian motion**. This is the random movement of things like pollen grains suspended in water, which can be seen under a microscope. Einstein proved it was caused by water molecules hitting the pollen, thus showing that molecules (and hence atoms) are real, physical objects and not, as some thought at the time, mere abstractions.

27. They are the **names of atomic orbitals**. Electrons, being governed by quantum theory, are simultaneously waves and particles, and their precise position is always uncertain. They do not, therefore, orbit atomic nuclei in the way that planets orbit the sun. Rather, they are more or less likely to be found in a particular, often lobe-shaped, volume of space near the nucleus.

 28. A **neutron star**, or **pulsar**. In 1992 it became the first star other than the sun to be confirmed as having planets orbiting it.

29. 60. Their arrangement is the same as that of the vertices of the polygons that make up a football.

30. **Oxygen**. All elements heavier than lithium (some of which, along with hydrogen and helium, was synthesised in the Big Bang) are entirely the product of atomic-fusion reactions inside stars or of stellar explosions called supernovae. Lighter elements are generally more abundant, but the details of these reactions conspire to favour oxygen.

31. In the atmosphere. It is a layer of ionised gas that reflects radio waves, meaning they can be detected over the horizon from where they are broadcast.

32. Ageing. The idea is that, since accident or disease will carry an organism off eventually, it is not worth evolution investing too heavily in bodily repair mechanisms, if those resources might better be deployed in reproduction. Hence the soma (ie, the body) is disposable.

33. Venera 7, a Soviet probe, which arrived on Venus in 1970.

34. Mercury. There is no particular known reason as to why this is so. It just is.

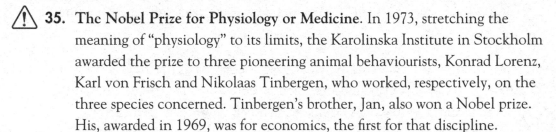 **35. The Nobel Prize for Physiology or Medicine**. In 1973, stretching the meaning of "physiology" to its limits, the Karolinska Institute in Stockholm awarded the prize to three pioneering animal behaviourists, Konrad Lorenz, Karl von Frisch and Nikolaas Tinbergen, who worked, respectively, on the three species concerned. Tinbergen's brother, Jan, also won a Nobel prize. His, awarded in 1969, was for economics, the first for that discipline.

36. Aldabra, an atoll in the Indian Ocean. Their habitation of the place helped save it from being turned into a military base in the 1960s.

37. **Ammonia**, which, in turn, is made into fertiliser and explosives, and which helps explain why the 20th century saw both the greatest population growth in history, and the bloodiest wars.

38. **Comets.** This cloud, which surrounds the sun and is believed to stretch out for around a light year, contains frozen leftovers from the solar system's beginning. Occasionally, one of these falls in towards the sun, developing a tail of gas and dust as it heats up on the way.

39. **Asteroids that have the same orbit as Jupiter.** The Greeks orbit 30 degrees in front of the planet and the Trojans 30 degrees behind it. These locations, called Lagrange points, are places where the combined gravities of Jupiter and the sun create a "well" from which objects, once inside, cannot easily escape.

40. **Its reaction to a violet stain**, which was discovered in the 19th century by Christian Gram, a Danish bacteriologist. Gram-positive bacteria retain the stain. Gram-negative ones do not. In general, Gram-negative bacteria are more resistant to antibiotics.

41. **Polonium**—named after her native land, Poland.

42. **Mimicry.** A Batesian mimic is an edible animal species that looks like a poisonous one, to fool predators into leaving it alone. A Mullerian mimic is a poisonous animal species that looks like another poisonous one, making it easier for predators to learn what to leave alone. And a Vavilovian mimic is a weed that looks like a crop, fooling farmers into leaving it alone.

43. **A piece of natural glass** created by molten rock splashed out by a meteorite strike. Most are found within one of four fields, each associated with a single strike, in Australasia, North America, Central Europe and the Ivory Coast.

44. **A piece of tissue** in which the cell membranes have disappeared, leaving a mass of cytoplasm with nuclei floating free in it. Many fungi are syncytia. And several viruses cause pathological syncytia to form.

45. **The two arms of the molecule around a carbon-carbon double bond.** Carbon atoms can bond to four neighbouring atoms, but in some circumstances they bond twice to the same atom, forming a double bond. Single bonds can rotate, but double bonds are rigid, helping define a molecule's geometry. All fats have long chains of linked carbon atoms in them. In a cis fat, a double bond puts a kink in this chain. In a trans fat it does not.

46. **The chance of there being intelligent, industrial life elsewhere in the galaxy.** The equation has terms for the number of stars in the galaxy, the fraction with habitable planets, the likelihood of life emerging on a planet,

and so on. Some terms have plausible numbers attached. Others do not. It was devised in 1961, by Frank Drake, an American astronomer.

47. **A telescope**. Specifically, one that always pointed at the sky's zenith. Besides being an architect, Christopher Wren, who designed the monument, was also an astronomer.

48. It is the **chemical cycle** by which plants use energy derived from light to turn water and carbon dioxide into sugar and oxygen.

49. **1950**. Establishing the age of an object often requires radioactive dating. For objects more recent than 1950 that is hard, because they may have been contaminated by radioactivity from bomb tests.

50. **Isaac Newton**, in an uncharacteristic (and probably calculated) bout of modesty.

LITERARY DEVICES: Books and arts

1. a) **Dance** b) **astronomy** c) **history**.

2. a) *The Joy Luck Club* by **Amy Tan** b) *The Secret History* by **Donna Tartt** c) *The Color Purple* by **Alice Walker** d) *The Poisonwood Bible* by **Barbara Kingsolver**.

3. a) *Flaubert's Parrot* by **Julian Barnes** b) *Cloud Atlas* by **David Mitchell** c) *London Fields* by **Martin Amis** d) *The Reluctant Fundamentalist* by **Mohsin Hamid**.

 4. a) **Agatha Christie** b) **Benjamin Franklin** (he used a variety of pen names) c) **C. S. Lewis** d) **Anne Brontë**.

5. a) **El Greco** b) **Caravaggio** c) **Mark Chagall** d) **Donatello**.

6. a) **Seamus Heaney** b) **Dario Fo** c) **Doris Lessing** d) **Derek Walcott**.

7. a) **Dave Eggers** b) **Haruki Murakami** c) **David Foster Wallace** d) **Thomas Pynchon**.

8. a) **Harlan Coben** b) **Lee Child** c) **James Patterson** d) **Michael Connelly**.

9. a) **Sweden** b) **Norway** c) **Denmark**.

10. a) **Jo Nesbo** b) **Henning Mankell** c) **Karin Fossum**.

11. a) **Cornelius Vanderbilt**—the author of the winner in 2010 was T. J. Stiles. b) **Andrew Jackson**—Jon Meacham won the prize in 2009. c) **Robert Oppenheimer**—Kai Bird and Martin J. Sherwin were the joint winners in 2006.

12. a) **John Rawls**. The book argued that if people had to choose a society through a "veil of ignorance" (not knowing what their position in society would be) they would choose a system based on political liberty and equality of opportunity. b) **Francis Fukuyama**. As the Berlin Wall fell, Fukuyama argued that liberal democracy had "won" the argument as to the best form of society. c) **Edward Said**. Said argued that western depictions of eastern society were patronising and designed to demonstrate the superiority of the western model.

13. a) **Children's literature** b) **science fiction and fantasy** c) **poetry, specifically American poets**. At $100,000, the Ruth Lilly prize is one of the most lucrative literary awards.

14. **Albert Camus**. De Beauvoir won for *Les Mandarins* in 1954, Proust for *A l'ombre des jeunes filles en fleurs* in 1919 and Houellebecq for *La Carte et le Territoire* in 2010.

15. a) **William Faulkner** b) **Harper Lee** c) **Anthony Trollope**.

16. a) **Edward Estlin** b) **Vidiadhar Surajprasad** c) **Antonia Susan** d) **Thomas Stearns**.

17. *Don Quixote*, with around 500 million copies sold. Miguel de Cervantes's satire about a deluded knight was first published in 1612 and is still regarded as one of the best novels ever written.

18. a) **Hereford cathedral** b) **the Shrine of the Book, Israel Museum, Jerusalem** c) **Trinity College, Dublin**.

19. a) *The Diary of Anne Frank* b) **The Beatles** c) *Lord of the Flies* by William Golding d) *À la recherche du temps perdu* by Marcel Proust.

20. a) *101 Dalmatians* b) *The Sound of Music* c) *The Sixth Sense* (bit of a spoiler, this one) and d) *The Matrix*.

 21. **Sylvester Stallone** and **Madonna**.

22. a) **John Alcott**—the film is noted for the early use of Steadicam. Stanley Kubrick directed. b) **Gunnar Fischer**—a long-time collaborator with Ingmar Bergman. c) **Gregg Toland**—the look of this Orson Welles classic is one reason why it is often voted the greatest movie of all time.

23. Italy with 11.

24. Nigeria. The term may have been coined by a writer at *The Economist*, Matt Steinglass, when at the *New York Times*. The industry is the second-largest employer in Nigeria, with 1 million workers.

25. *Gone with the Wind*, from back in 1939. *Avatar* is the top-grossing film in nominal terms. James Cameron (*Avatar* and *Titanic*) and Steven Spielberg (*ET* and *Jaws*) each have two of the top 10.

26. e) *Twister*, which starred Bill Paxton and Helen Hunt.

27. a) **Greer Garson** b) **Keira Knightley** c) **Jennifer Ehle.**

28. *Bridget Jones's Diary*, an adaptation of Helen Fielding's novel of the same name.

29. a) *Heart of Darkness* by Joseph Conrad. The film, directed by Francis Ford Coppola, was a troubled production; a documentary called *Heart of Darkness* was later made about it. b) *Far from the Madding Crowd* by Thomas

Hardy. The novel was adapted into a cartoon by Posy Simmonds, which was turned into the film. c) *Emma* by Jane Austen.

30. a) *Cheers* b) *Breaking Bad* c) *Beverly Hills 90210*.

31. a) *Sanford and Son* b) *All in the Family* c) *Three's Company*.

32. a) **The Louvre**, Paris b) **The Prado**, Madrid c) **The Uffizi**, Florence d) **Rijksmuseum**, Amsterdam.

33. a) **Film** b) **painting** c) **ceramics/pottery**.

34. **St Petersburg in 1904**. He graduated from the Imperial Ballet School before leaving for Paris in 1921 and eventually moving to the United States in 1933.

35. **The Blue period**.

36. a) **Vincent van Gogh** b) **Henri Matisse** c) **Paul Cézanne**.

37. a) **Johannes Vermeer**. The artist was played by Colin Firth. b) **Michaelangelo**. Charlton Heston played the artist as he painted the Sistine Chapel. c) **Vincent van Gogh**, who was played by Kirk Douglas while Anthony Quinn won an Oscar for playing Paul Gauguin.

38. a) **Alexander Calder** b) **Marcel Duchamp** c) **Henry Moore**.

39. a) **Renzo Piano** b) **Frank Gehry** c) **Zaha Hadid**.

40. a) **Rococo** b) **Baroque** c) **Gothic**.

41. The **Antoinette Perry Award** for Excellence in Broadway Theatre.

42. a) **Christian and Gospel** b) **Music of Black Origin** c) **Latin music**.

43. a) *A Midsummer Night's Dream* b) *Measure for Measure* c) *The Winter's Tale*.

44. a) *Antony and Cleopatra* b) *Twelfth Night* c) *As You Like It*.

45. a) *Macbeth* as directed by Akira Kurosawa; the plot is transferred to feudal Japan. b) *The Taming of the Shrew*. The Cole Porter musical is set among the cast of Shakespeare's play and includes the song "Brush Up Your Shakespeare". c) *Twelfth Night* is remade in this movie as a college-based romcom.

46. a) **Richard Rodgers and Oscar Hammerstein** b) **John Kander and Fred Ebb** c) **Leonard Bernstein and Stephen Sondheim**.

47. a) *The Barber of Seville* by Rossini b) **Rigoletto** by Verdi c) **La Bohème** by Puccini.

48. a) **"We Didn't Start the Fire"** by Billy Joel b) **"Young Americans"** by David Bowie c) **"Money's Too Tight to Mention"** by Simply Red.

49. The soundtrack of **West Side Story**, the musical, was number 1 for 54 weeks.

50. **Dark Side of the Moon** by Pink Floyd with a remarkable 928 weeks, or almost 18 years, had the longest run, and the **Rolling Stones** with 37 had the most. To show the American public's diverse taste, Barbra Streisand and Frank Sinatra had 34 and 33 top 10 albums respectively.

PublicAffairs is a publishing house founded in 1997. It is a tribute to the standards, values, and flair of three persons who have served as mentors to countless reporters, writers, editors, and book people of all kinds, including me.

I. F. STONE, proprietor of *I. F. Stone's Weekly*, combined a commitment to the First Amendment with entrepreneurial zeal and reporting skill and became one of the great independent journalists in American history. At the age of eighty, Izzy published *The Trial of Socrates*, which was a national bestseller. He wrote the book after he taught himself ancient Greek.

BENJAMIN C. BRADLEE was for nearly thirty years the charismatic editorial leader of *The Washington Post*. It was Ben who gave the *Post* the range and courage to pursue such historic issues as Watergate. He supported his reporters with a tenacity that made them fearless and it is no accident that so many became authors of influential, best-selling books.

ROBERT L. BERNSTEIN, the chief executive of Random House for more than a quarter century, guided one of the nation's premier publishing houses. Bob was personally responsible for many books of political dissent and argument that challenged tyranny around the globe. He is also the founder and longtime chair of Human Rights Watch, one of the most respected human rights organizations in the world.

· · ·

For fifty years, the banner of Public Affairs Press was carried by its owner Morris B. Schnapper, who published Gandhi, Nasser, Toynbee, Truman, and about 1,500 other authors. In 1983, Schnapper was described by *The Washington Post* as "a redoubtable gadfly." His legacy will endure in the books to come.

Peter Osnos, *Founder*